Transforming
SCHOOL CLIMATE
and
LEARNING

To the teachers and students, who together can transform themselves, their schools, and the world.

Transforming
SCHOOL CLIMATE
and
LEARNING

BEYOND BULLYING AND COMPLIANCE

BILL PREBLE   RICK GORDON
Foreword by Raymond J. McNulty

CORWIN
A SAGE Company

CORWIN
A SAGE Company

FOR INFORMATION:

Corwin
A SAGE Company
2455 Teller Road
Thousand Oaks, California 91320
(800) 233-9936
Fax: (800) 417-2466
www.corwin.com

SAGE Ltd.
1 Oliver's Yard
55 City Road
London EC1Y 1SP
United Kingdom

SAGE India Pvt. Ltd.
B 1/I 1 Mohan Cooperative Industrial Area
Mathura Road, New Delhi 110 044
India

SAGE Asia-Pacific Pte. Ltd.
33 Pekin Street #02-01
Far East Square
Singapore 048763

Acquisitions Editor: Debra Stollenwerk
Associate Editor: Desirée A. Bartlett
Editorial Assistant: Kimberly Greenberg
Production Editor: Cassandra Margaret Seibel
Copy Editor: Gretchen Treadwell
Typesetter: C&M Digitals (P) Ltd.
Proofreader: Theresa Kay
Indexer: Gloria Tierney
Cover Designer: Michael Dubowe
Permissions Editor: Adele Hutchinson

Printed in the United States of America

Library of Congress Cataloging-in-Publication Data

Preble, William, 1953-

Transforming School Climate and Learning : beyond bullying and compliance / Bill Preble, Rick Gordon; foreword by Raymond J. McNulty.

p. cm.
Includes bibliographical references and index.

ISBN 978-1-4129-9268-8 (pbk.)

1. Bullying in schools. 2. School violence. I. Gordon, Rick. II. Title.

LB3013.3.P73 2011

371.5'8—dc22

2011006719

This book is printed on acid-free paper.

11 12 13 14 15 10 9 8 7 6 5 4 3 2 1

Contents

Foreword

We live in an educational environment obsessed with test scores, control, and predictability, and because of this, we build most school improvement plans around quantitative (hard) data gleaned from test results in core curriculum areas. We design solutions to poor student performance around specific content weaknesses that we see in the data, and then we launch the solution and wait to see the performance rise.

Although as educators we know the important influence that classroom and school climate has on student learning, climate gets little attention in school improvement plans. This has never been more evident to me than in the last five years as I have worked with some of the nation's most highly successful and rapidly improving schools for the International Center for Leadership in Education. All of these schools have challenging demographics (high poverty, etc.) yet their performance is near or at the top in their state.

I have spent time in these schools talking with students and asking them two key questions: "What makes a teacher worth listening to?" and "What makes a school worth going to?" Just a few years ago, I was in a large urban high school that was the lowest performing in the state and now was ranked at the top of all the urban schools. When I asked a student, "What makes this school worth going to?" his answer was simple and direct: "In this school, it's not us against them!" He went on to say that students had a voice in his school and that when problems emerged, they (students and teachers) solved them together.

Educators have understood for a long time that school climate has an enormous impact on learning and in the pages that follow, the case will be made.

Bill Preble and Rick Gordon have been quietly and effectively transforming schools into powerful learning communities without a lot of fanfare and expense for a long while. I got to know them when I was the commissioner of education in Vermont, and I have continued to follow their work while at the Gates Foundation and now at the International Center for Leadership in Education. They transform schools by empowering students, staff, and the community. The process they use to create such success is what I call *leadership density.*

I feel a strong connection to their work because they see leadership as I see it, not as a position but rather as a disposition for taking action, and that is what this book accomplishes. *Transforming School Climate and Learning* provides a road map that can turn students and educators from objects of change to agents of change, empowered to transform their schools.

Raymond J. McNulty
President
International Center for Leadership in Education

Acknowledgments

Deep appreciation goes to my colleagues at Main Street Academix and the Center for School Climate and Learning: Larry Taylor, Katie Knowles, Rachael Frost, Holly Preble, Bryan Partridge, Rick Gordon, and Chris Overtree. This process would not have been as finely tuned, nor as painstakingly researched and field tested, without your wisdom, dedication, and passion for the work. Thanks also to my colleagues and students from New England College (NEC), who traveled to schools doing this work alongside us, and put up with stories about respectful schools for over a decade.

We are grateful to the many teachers, students, and schools leaders who have worked so hard to stand up for civility, respect for all, and creative teaching in an age of NCLB standardization. Special thanks to Kevin Jennings, John O'Dell, Jack and Janie Barnes, Midge McPherson, Mike Hermann, Jane Slayton, Steve Wessler, Leo Corriveau and the many superintendents, principals, and student leaders from Tennessee, Maine, New Hampshire, Florida, and Massachusetts who've supported and implemented this process. You have helped us all better understand the important links between school safety, student leadership, school climate, and learning.

I wish to thank my coauthor and friend Rick Gordon, founder of the Compass School, educator, and writer extraordinaire. The school you created, one that so clearly embodies "the spirit, methods, and discipline of a free society," was found to have the highest school climate scores of any school we evaluated. It is truly a model for others to follow. When my NEC students visit Compass School each semester, on the bus ride home they nearly all exclaim, "Why wasn't my school like that? If I went to a school like Compass, I would be a different person . . . that's the kind of school I want to teach in!" Thanks Rick to you and your colleagues for building this wonderful school, for sharing your work in the pages that follow, and for being such a valued partner in writing this book.

Finally, the SafeMeasures™ Process and this book would not have been possible without the sacrifice and support of my family—Holly,

Christopher, and AnnaLi Preble—and Rick's family—Elaine, Manya, and Koby Gordon. Your patience, love, editorial suggestions, and insights are what made this possible.

Bill Preble, January 2, 2011

PUBLISHER'S ACKNOWLEDGMENTS

Corwin would like to thank the following individuals for their editorial insight:

Martin J. Hudacs, Superintendent
Solanco School District
Quarryville, PA

Cathy Patterson, Fifth-Grade Teacher and Former Assistant Principal
Evergreen Elementary School
Walnut Valley USD
Walnut, CA

Lyne Ssebikindu, Assistant Principal
Crump Elementary School
Memphis, TN

Gary L. Willhite, Professor
University of Wisconsin La Crosse
La Crosse, WI

About the Authors

Bill Preble earned an EdD from the University of Maine in curriculum and instruction and youth political socialization, and his MEd in social studies education from the University of Washington. He is a professor of education at New England College in Henniker, New Hampshire, where he teaches graduate and undergraduate courses in educational psychology, curriculum, and instruction; educational leadership; and school climate research, leadership, and facilitation.

He created Main Street Academix in 2001 and founded the Center for School Climate and Learning in 2010. These centers provide school climate research, evaluation services, and professional development on school climate leadership to schools and state departments of education throughout the country. He and his colleagues offer schools on-site school climate improvement services and support for implementation of the SafeMeasures™ Process, which offers a systemic, data-driven approach to preventing bullying and improving school climate and learning.

Bill has made hundreds of presentations on his research and school climate work at schools and professional conferences. He is the coauthor of *The Respectful School: How Educators and Students Can Conquer Hate and Harassment*, with Stephen Wessler (2003), and author of several articles on school climate leadership and bullying prevention.

Bill and his wife Holly have two teenaged children, Christopher and AnnaLi. He enjoys spending time at his cottage in Maine, playing racquetball, and playing the drums anywhere, anytime he can.

 **Rick Gordon** has a PhD in social and multicultural foundations of education from the University of Colorado–Boulder, a MEd from the University of Minnesota in political science with a focus on organizational theory and public policy, and graduated from Stanford University with honors in political science. He was founding director of Compass School, a Grade 7–12 school that has scored highest on a national survey on respect, safety, and school climate. Rick codirected the Critical Skills/Education by Design Program at Antioch New England Graduate School, where he also was on the education department faculty, and has worked extensively with schools and higher education on service learning (including editing the well-received *Problem Based Service Learning Fieldguide: Making a Difference in Higher Education*). Rick has been a humanities teacher, run several small businesses, and had the honor of visiting thousands of classrooms as an educational ethnographer and consultant over the years. He continues to be involved in teacher development and teaches courses in school leadership in various locales. He has long experience in experiential education with Outward Bound and Interlochen and has traveled extensively around the globe leading programs for youth. He played college soccer and continues his commitment to learning through sports as a coach of youth soccer and Nordic skiing.

Introduction

Bringing Our Schools Into Balance

Good teachers understand that when students feel stressed, threatened, angry, or unsafe, they are less likely to learn. Every new teacher learns the importance of meeting basic human needs for safety and belonging (Maslow, 1968). Teachers who are familiar with the latest research on the dynamics of the brain know that clarity of academic thinking can be impeded when we are under emotional stress or duress (Jensen, 2008a).

This book aims to make a research-based case for the importance of school climate, not only to support the social and emotional well-being of students, but because we believe the only way to achieve and sustain strong academic results is through the interaction between positive school climate and learning.

Schools are not always the safest, most respectful places, especially for any child who may appear to be remotely "different." For many students, school can be a mean, lonely, irrelevant, even dangerous place. As many as 73 percent of all students report being directly or indirectly exposed to bullies in school (Rivers, Poteat, Noret, & Ashurts, 2009). Perhaps this is why the recent attention to the problem of bullying is resonating so widely and powerfully through our culture. Most of us have either experienced it personally or we've seen it happening all too frequently to friends or family members.

For the past decade or more, since the school shootings at Columbine, issues of school safety have been front and center in schools and communities across the country. Safety plans, lockdown drills, and evacuation plans have been created and we have seen firsthand how these school safety plans can be effective tools for saving lives. But no school safety plan alone will ensure that a school is completely physically and emotionally safe. A school without guns is a fine goal, but it is not necessarily a safe school nor a learning school.

BEYOND BULLYING, BEYOND COMPLIANCE

The tragedy and injustice of bullying is finally becoming clear to educators, parents, school officials, and state leaders. While new anti-bullying laws, better school policies, and zero-tolerance disciplinary models may be a welcome attempt to ensure that adults begin to more fully address the suffering, humiliation, and social isolation imposed by bullies, in our view, they will not solve these complex problems. We know that all too often such new initiatives in our schools amount to little more than window dressing that fails to address deeper, more systemic problems. Despite all the media attention being paid to bullying, the problem facing schools today is not simply a problem of bad kids (e.g., bullies). Rather, the fundamental issue in schools relates to the overall school climate that encompasses not just bullying and student discipline but the whole relationship of students and adults to school and learning.

The issue of bullying is a symptom of larger social, emotional, and systemic educational problems. When educators aim to make their schools safer, more respectful places, it often follows a focus on achieving higher levels of "student compliance." The underlying belief seems to be, "If those darned kids just did what they were told [by adults] then everything would be okay!"

In the chapters that follow, we will challenge this assumption that safer, more respectful schools are simply places with more rules, harsher penalties for violators, fewer behavior problems, and where kids do just as they are told. Of course, rules are important. But we will show how schools that empower students and partner with them to define, assess, and implement what we refer to as *respectful teaching and school practices* are those that achieve real results for school climate and learning.

School climate is the combined result of the

- Quality of the relationships (both adult and student) within a school
- School's overarching vision, goals, and mission
- Systems of support for students, teachers, and parents that enable the school to achieve its mission
- Roles available to and played by students, teachers, and school leaders
- Opportunities for active, meaningful engagement as learners, leaders, and citizens within the school and community
- Extent to which there is respect, tolerance, fairness, equity, and social justice at every level of the school's culture

The quality of a school's climate goes far beyond "getting the kids to behave" and "comply" with adult demands. In schools that have a positive climate, there is a purposeful vision and systemic mission to link positive school climate and learning. Teachers and students are partners in creating a school culture that values each individual, engages all in learning, and actively supports the success of every member of the community. The school values and promotes civic engagement and service to the larger community. Everyone—adults and students—is an active agent of fairness, social justice, and change. Schools that recognize the limits of compliance and include their students in the process of school improvement are a special brand of schools.

GETTING BEYOND PIECEMEAL PROBLEM SOLVING

There is no doubting the good intentions to improve schools—bullying and harassment prevention programs, school security officers, video cameras in school buses, test preparation programs, diversity training, dropout prevention, lunchroom monitors, curriculum mapping, reading specialists, curriculum consultants . . . There is no shortage of problems in schools (or any place where hundreds or thousands of people are put together day after day, year after year). And for every problem, schools offer a well-intended solution usually involving some new program, policy, or staff position. But like the carnival game of Whac-A-Mole, when a problem is pushed down in one place, a new problem seems to jump up somewhere else.

This common and never-ending strategy of identifying individual problems to solve one at a time, exerting our best efforts as wise and experienced adults, hasn't, as yet, eradicated problems in schools. In fact, our concerted efforts to raise test scores may be exacerbating other problems—narrowing the curriculum, sapping the joy of learning, ignoring developmental needs, lessening time for physical activity, pushing out struggling students, raising stress levels for teachers and students, and instead of valuing the whole child, students can be reduced to mere test results as part of subgroups on the big NCLB scorecard.

This approach to using "expert" (read adult) knowledge to try to solve school problems ignores the basics of what we know about human nature and the change process. Endless experience supports the age-old wisdom, you can lead a horse to water but you can't make it drink—reform imposed from above rarely sticks. Our deepest educational thinkers—such as Michael Fullan, Seymour Sarason, and John Goodlad—marshal a lifetime of research showing the futility of top-down reform. Change does not happen from the outside; change is not something that can be imposed on people. In human institutions such as schools, lasting and meaningful change must come from within the school, employing the primary resource schools have—the energy, ideas, expertise, and goodwill of every individual in the school community.

Our experience as educators and our research with schools has demonstrated the power of positive school climate to simultaneously improve school safety and academic achievement. In fact, the case we wish to make is that the only way to sustain improvement in academic achievement is to improve school climate and culture for faculty and students in the school. Unless students feel safe at school, feel a sense of belonging, and feel valued in the learning process, it is unlikely we will see students perform anywhere close to their potential. For too long, schools have separated issues related to academic results from those tied to school violence, student relations, and respect. We have found, in our work with schools throughout the nation, that these issues are inextricably linked—improve respect in schools and learning improves. Without respectful and safe schools, the learning environment is compromised.

As schools wrestle with pressing issues of improving academic performance while also trying to stop bullying and other ways students mistreat each other, why does anyone need a book on school climate? Certainly there is an urgent need to respond to egregious and dangerous student behavior to assure every child is physically safe. But if all we do about bullying is develop more stringent policies, exert more adult authority, and increase consequences for misbehavior, it is not only unlikely there will be a substantive decrease in school violence, but we may worsen other problems. By framing problem solving under the unifying umbrella of school climate, schools can address immediate problems while elevating the overall health of the school and developing organizational capacity to continue the ongoing work of school improvement.

Our studies show that adults and students often share similar desires for their school. They can clearly understand the things that are working well and the things that aren't. The way we see it, in many cases, teachers and students are the real experts on the school experience—they know all too well what does and doesn't work in their schools. They have dreams (and all too fleeting moments of experience) of what really does work to promote learning for every child. While understanding research and "best practices" can help, what matters is the ability of local teachers, leaders, parents, community members, and students to articulate and name their problems and the solutions that they then embrace.

This book aims to make a research-based case for the importance of school climate, not only to support the social and emotional well-being of students but—and this is the most essential argument of the book—also because we believe the only way to achieve and sustain strong academic results is through the interaction between positive school climate, student engagement, respectful caring relationships, empowerment, and learning. We believe that this book will help school leaders make the powerful and important connection between improving school climate and improving the quality of teaching and learning in a school.

THE RATIONALE FOR THIS BOOK: SCHOOL CLIMATE AS A KEY TO SCHOOL SAFETY, STUDENT MOTIVATION, AND ACADEMIC ACHIEVEMENT

The idea that we can somehow ignore the social and emotional aspects of schooling is just plain silly. Yet, this is precisely what many schools have done for nearly a decade under No Child Left Behind (NCLB) and during similar periods of our history in public education. We are convinced that the time is now ripe for refocusing our attention on school climate, safety, and respect and the important effects that these have on students' personal, intellectual, social, and civic development.

We welcome the fact that educational leaders and teachers are beginning to adopt a more balanced perspective about the things that truly matter in education. There is increasing interest in unifying what we know about human dignity, freedom, happiness, and leadership in complex systems like schools with what we know about the conditions in which human beings thrive and grow.

This is not some recycled "touchy-feely" school reform agenda. Its roots can be found deep within the humanistic traditions of our culture and are tied directly to the compelling new research on human development, the brain, and what we now understand about how people learn.

We think school climate is like the air we breathe or the soil in which we plant a seed to grow. Both the air and the soil provide something that is essential to growth and to life. Learning cannot be achieved in the midst of a hostile, threatening environment. As Jerome Freiberg (1999), an eminent researcher in the field of school climate research, says, "Much like the air we breathe, school climate is ignored until it becomes foul" (p. 1). We are all too familiar with the results of toxic school environments. School shootings such as Columbine (U.S. Secret Service, 2002) and the more recent tragedies at South Hadley and Virginia Tech can all be linked to the impact of bullying and an alienating school environment.

In recent years, forty-four states have adopted tough new anti-bullying laws in response to the increased recognition of this problem in schools. We know from conversations with Kevin Jennings, assistant deputy secretary for Safe and Drug-Free Schools for the U.S. Department of Education, that the Title IV program formerly dedicated to "safe and drug-free schools" has been reframed to focus on evaluating and improving school climate. Under the new safe schools model, all schools will soon be asked to evaluate school climate from both student and adult perspectives, in addition to academic achievement, and assess how well they are meeting the social, emotional, and educational needs of their students and the needs of their communities. There will be a new kind of accountability to make our schools places where all students feel safe and respected by their teachers and peers.

Our research on respectful schools has shown us that it is the daily acts of kindness and appreciation shown to others that begin to frame school experiences for both students and adults. It is the relationships between teachers and learners, high expectations coupled with adult support, the availability of choices and options, and opportunities for each person's ideas to be heard and valued that have powerful effects on creating respectful schools.

It is difficult to go one day, it seems, without hearing the latest news report about bullying, school violence, school discipline problems, the untenable drop-out rate, and the need to re-engage disinterested learners in our nation's schools. All of these issues relate to school climate and the need to make our schools more personalized, more interesting, engaging, exciting, and meaningful places for our youth.

It is increasingly clear that our schools need to change. Every day, young people come home from schools that have all too often been devoid of engagement, excitement, meaningful choices, and higher-order thinking. At a time when the sheer volume of knowledge; the pace of technological innovation; and highly complex, global, social, economic, cultural, and political problems are growing exponentially, we should by no means be narrowing the curriculum so that we can ensure students pass a simplistic set of standardized tests. Instead, our children need to be expanding their reach, their understanding, and their ability to meet the challenges of the twenty-first century.

The skills needed for the modern world go far beyond the basic knowledge and skills that most state testing demands. In a rapidly changing global economy, our graduates need the skills of problem solving, communication, critical thinking, adaptability, and collaboration (Wagner, 2008). When we focus solely on academic achievement outcomes, we can often lose sight of what is most important—our students and what they need to assure their success. This curricular narrowing not only fails to meet the needs of the twenty-first century, but it also makes our schools less and less engaging for students. Too many students are being left behind as pressures of testing sap much of the energy from the classroom and push many students out of the ever more confining system.

At a time when every child needs a strong and broad education to be prepared for democratic community life, and when students need ever more diverse skills for the dynamic world of the twenty-first century, the narrow focus on test scores and academics is often more limiting than liberating. At best, students may be gaining basic factual knowledge and basic skills. Too often, students are simply becoming better test takers, or even worse, being turned off on learning and school by a curriculum that feels far removed from the needs of the twenty-first century.

GUIDEPOSTS FOR SCHOOL LEADERS: ADMINISTRATORS, TEACHERS, *AND* STUDENTS

Balancing Leadership Roles and Voices

The central purpose of this book is to help school leaders improve school climate and learning through the engagement of student leaders and teachers. Using positive peer pressure from a diverse team of student leaders, along with collaborative action research, schools can develop the capacity for sustained improvement in school climate and, as a result, improvements in learning.

This book is designed to help school leaders reestablish the equilibrium that seems to have been lost in our schools. We make the case that schools must balance the push for high academic achievement with understanding that academic rigor will not be accomplished without providing a safe and respectful learning environment—a positive school climate—for all students in our schools.

The foundational structure we use for school climate improvement we call SafeMeasures™, a collaborative action research process developed by William Preble and his colleagues at Main Street Academix that has been successfully used in hundreds of schools across the United States over the last decade to improve school climate, expand leadership roles, and improve teaching and learning. We use the label of SafeMeasures throughout the book as one example of a well-structured collaborative action research process that can be applied to build organizational capacity in any setting. SafeMeasures focuses on both of the following:

1. A leadership model that includes students and teachers working together to collect and analyze school data

2. An action planning and implementation process that results in changes at the school and classroom level to impact climate and learning

The stages of SafeMeasures detailed in the following chapters are the following:

Stage One: Everyone is a leader: Empowering students and teachers. This chapter shows how to establish a design team to lead the process that includes students and teachers.

Stage Two: Including all voices: School climate data collection. This chapter demonstrates strategies for collecting qualitative and quantitative school climate data in a school.

Stage Three: Thinking together: Data analysis and goal setting. This chapter explains how data are used to "change people's minds" about their school's strengths and needs, and how to use data to develop school climate and learning improvement goals.

Stage Four: Making change happen: Action planning and project development. This chapter shows educators how to use the Respect Continuum and a list of research-based action projects to develop a powerful school improvement culture that will dramatically change school climate and student engagement in learning.

Stage Five: Moving forward together: Sustainability and continuous improvement. This chapter explains how student leadership and engagement can drive the school improvement process in any school, especially when school climate projects align with academic learning goals.

ORGANIZATION OF THE BOOK

The book is framed around this five-stage process, including leadership team development, data collection and analysis, goal setting, action planning, and sustained school change. The first two chapters lay out the case for school climate and the role of teachers and students as partners in the change process. Chapters 3–6 and 8 detail each stage of the SafeMeasures process, offering not only practical approaches for facilitation but also concrete examples of SafeMeasures in action. In each chapter, we share what we hope are inspiring stories and effective practices of school climate improvement to provide a template for readers to impact climate in their own setting.

These core chapters are organized to be both informative and practical. Each chapter

- Explains the rationale for the particular stage of the process, along with step-by-step procedures to allow readers to implement the process in their own setting
- Is elucidated with a story of "making it real" to show how this stage looks in action, in real school settings
- Concludes with a summary to offer a succinct "how-to" overview of the stage

- Provides book study questions at the end to guide the reader's own reflection and application of these ideas and to encourage shared reflection within a professional learning community

Because the vast majority of a student's time in school is spent in the classroom, we dedicate Chapter 7 to the critical pillar of engaged teaching and learning. School climate must involve more than just respect in the hallways and lunchroom. The focus of schools ultimately needs to be on the learning environment, and how this embodies the values of social and emotional safety, valuing of every individual, and a culture of respect can profoundly influence the climate of the school. Chapter 7 offers an array of best practices we have seen work in schools that engage students in the learning process and reflect an ethic of respectful teaching and learning.

Chapter 9 concludes the book with consideration of how a focus on school climate can provide a central, organizing framework for all other school improvement initiatives not only in individual schools but also on a more systemic level.

WHY READ THIS BOOK?

There is no shortage of literature talking about how to improve American education. Some offer practical solutions aimed at particular problems but fail to address the structural and cultural conditions that can undermine implementation of these ideas. Other books suggest revamping schools or the educational system and might offer a future direction but do little to address the immediate challenges confronting educators daily.

This book aims to reframe the dialogue from

- Piecemeal programs aimed at individual issues to a more holistic approach that creates the underlying conditions in the school climate and culture to subsequently help schools address the array of challenges and goals they face
- A limiting and futile focus on simply eliminating unacceptable behaviors to more liberating and expansive attention on how to teach, support, encourage, and honor positive behaviors
- Reacting to problems as they are identified to building organizational capacity for replicable processes that bring stakeholders together to effect and lead solutions for the challenges schools confront
- Reliance on "experts" from outside the school telling schools how to change to the experts inside the school leading the change
- A history of failed reforms and new initiatives to a sustainable model for continual school improvement

STUDENTS AND TEACHERS AS PARTNERS IN TRANSFORMING SCHOOL CLIMATE

As our research in schools throughout the United States has shown, when we move beyond a focus on stopping negative behavior and compliance with adult rules and dictates, and toward creating positive school climate, exciting new possibilities emerge. This occurs through focusing attention on the social and emotional well-being of every child (and adult), actively valuing each individual, and looking for ways to include all voices in the success of the school. Powerful effects ensue—producing fewer discipline problems, improving student motivation, and increasing student academic performance (Freiberg, 1999; Preble & Newman, 2006).

We make the case that students, even more so than adults, are often the real experts on school climate. Much of what constitutes or contributes to school climate happens, as one student told us, "When grown-ups aren't around." We show how schools can incorporate student and adult perspectives, and provide new leadership roles for teams of diverse students to serve as partners in school reform. Positive school climate, at its heart, is based on the value and dignity of every individual—SafeMeasures is designed to help schools focus more clearly on the unique perspectives and school experiences of all members of the school community.

We share success stories from schools across the country that are able to hold high academic expectations for all children while also creating the conditions and supports that enable each child to reach these expectations. This book showcases schools effectively balancing the *desired ends with the appropriate means* to meet the academic, social, and emotional needs of their students.

The central purpose of the book is to help school leaders improve school climate and learning through the collaborative action research process we call SafeMeasures—engaging student leaders and teachers in a process of collaborative, schoolwide inquiry and improvement. We have seen firsthand how the process of collecting school climate data, comparing teacher and student perceptions of school climate, and developing action plans and projects to improve school climate can bring a school together. We have also seen the simultaneous impact that improving school climate has on improving student learning.

This book is designed to share this process with educators and student leaders, and to help school leaders reestablish the equilibrium between these social, emotional, and academic dimensions of schooling.

1

School Climate

The Heart and Soul of a School

School climate is like the air we breathe—it tends to go unnoticed until something is seriously wrong.

Jerome Freiburg, *School Climate* (1999, p. 1)

MAKING MEANINGFUL IMPROVEMENT IN SCHOOLS

There are many problems confronting our schools—bullying and harassment, inadequate academic performance, children who feel left out or fall between the cracks, disrespectful behavior, unmotivated students, and frustrated teachers. Despite countless reform initiatives, "research-based" programs, mandates, school assemblies, and outside speakers, these challenges persist in many schools. This book is about not just taking steps to address school issues such as these, but about a sustainable problem-solving process—one that makes real progress on the targeted issue *while* building capacity within schools to address other challenges inherent to school life.

We make the case that piecemeal efforts, one-time assemblies, and off-the-shelf programs rarely get to the heart of the difficulties schools need to address. Whatever happens in schools happens in a context, a context that the school culture and climate influence and shape, and that can undermine even the best-intentioned ideas.

Without creating a more positive school climate, most efforts to institute change will flounder—maybe never getting off the ground, or lasting only as long as the program funding, or at best, being an isolated bright spot out of step with other parts of the school program.

This book focuses on school climate as the heart and soul of school success for both adults and students. It is this climate that creates the conditions for students, teachers, and administrators to work effectively—feeling safe and supported, able to make a difference through their efforts, and ready to contribute to the good of the school as a whole.

Whether aiming to prevent bullying, increase attendance, lessen disciplinary incidents, or improve academic performance, the umbrella of school climate offers a comprehensive framework for real problem solving and organizational capacity building. This is the orientation that facilitates continuous school improvement.

WHY IS SCHOOL CLIMATE IMPORTANT?

What would you do if your child came home from school upset that her peers called her names, threatened to hurt her, or made fun of her when she made mistakes in class? You would probably ask her what the grown-ups at school were doing to help her, right? What if she said that there was no adult at school that she felt comfortable talking to about these problems, and there was nobody at school she could turn to for help?

Would you expect that, after a while, she would become stressed and anxious about going to school? Do you think that her grades would eventually suffer? Would she be less and less eager to even go to school each day if nothing were to change?

If this were the case, then your daughter would not be alone. Our research (Preble & Knowles, 2011) on elementary school students shows that nearly one out of every five children (20 percent) report feeling physically or emotionally unsafe at school and the same number of students report that there is no adult they can turn to for help at school. In a class of twenty-five students, that means that at least five students feel unsafe and are typically dealing with it on their own.

An important study about bullying in school called the Youth Voice Project (Davis & Nixon, 2011) offers quite similar findings, as 22 percent of students in the elementary grades reported at least two incidences of peer victimization per month. These findings are consistent with those of Olweus (1993) in his seminal studies of bullying in schools.

Davis and Nixon (2011) also examined how students responded when their peers bullied them, and found that the vast majority of students "pretended it doesn't bother them" (75 percent), "told the person to stop" (71 percent), "told a friend" (71 percent), or "walked away" (66 percent). Only 42 percent of the students in the Youth Voice study told an adult at school. So, it should be no surprise that when we ask teachers to tell us how safe or respectful their schools are, the vast majority say that their schools are "just fine"—they seem safe and respectful places for students. These adults are likely unaware of the severity of the school climate problems that are happening in their schools.

Given the fact that most students don't report bullying incidents to adults at school, and that much of what contributes to peer victimization happens out of the direct view of adults, it is really no wonder that there is such a disconnect between what students understand about school climate and what grown-ups (i.e., teachers and administrators) believe is happening right under their noses. This disconnect presents a serious challenge. If adults honestly believe that these problems do not exist at their schools, how likely are they going to be to try to address them? Perhaps even more important, when adults do take up the challenge of addressing school climate issues, how effective can we expect them to be when most do not understand what is really going on?

PREVENTING PITFALLS: DON'T UNDERESTIMATE THE IMPORTANCE OF SCHOOL CLIMATE

Educators have been under increasing pressure for more than a decade to focus on student academic performance and test scores. Moving to a more balanced view of the importance of the learning environment, then, will take thoughtful advocacy. Reminding adults of the impact of stress and threat on performance, for adults in the workplace as well as students in the classroom, can help remind educators of the important connections between positive climate and performance.

Bullying and peer-to-peer harassment at school are not the only factors that influence school climate. The ways that teachers establish discipline and rules in classrooms affect school climate. The kind of relationships teachers develop with their students affects the climate within a classroom and a school. The teaching methods a teacher uses makes the classroom either an engaging place for learning or a dull setting that students can't wait to leave.

In the following chapters, we elaborate a process for engaging students as partners with adults to develop a shared understanding of the most serious school climate issues within their school. This common vision allows them to work together to take effective steps to address these concerns. Let's begin by looking in more depth at the reasons schools are now beginning to take issues of school climate more seriously.

SCHOOL CLIMATE AND EFFECTIVE SCHOOLS

School climate is not a new idea. In the 1980s, research on *effective schools* demonstrated the importance of providing a safe and orderly school environment (Edmonds, 1979; Walberg, 1984). More recently, the topic of school climate has received increased attention after being linked to school violence in reports by both the U.S. Department of Health and Human Services (2001) and the U.S. Secret Service (2002). School climate has been associated with nearly every incident involving school shootings reported over the past fifteen years. It seems quite clear that if teachers and school leaders pay too little attention to school climate problems, serious consequences may occur.

It is difficult, if not impossible, for most students to focus on learning when they have to deal with disrespect, bullying, harassment, public humiliation, hate speech, threats, or violence. A review of forty major studies between 1964 and 1980 found that over half of these studies reported important effects of school climate on student achievement (Anderson, 1982).

In our own research in thirty-six schools in Sullivan County, Tennessee, we found a nearly 10 percent increase in academic performance in those schools that made a significant improvement in school climate over a three year period (Preble & Newman, 2006). To plan for and monitor school improvement, the district has adopted a process of collecting school climate data each year along with its academic testing data. They obviously feel that school climate matters (Preble & Taylor, 2008).

There is a growing body of research showing how a positive school climate facilitates not only student learning and higher academic achievement but also promotes the healthy social and emotional development of students (Adelman & Taylor, 2005; Freiburg, 1999). Jonathan Cohen, director of the Center for Social and Emotional Education, cites a safe, positive climate for learning as one of the most important factors for schools to promote the kind of social, emotional, ethical, and academic education that is essential for participation in democracy. This safe, caring, engaging learning environment can be developed through systemic intervention and is essential "to provide the platform upon which we teach and learn" (Cohen & Elias, 2010).

School climate also contributes to risk prevention and to positive youth development. Stated simply, in schools where students experience a positive school climate, students are generally less at risk for antisocial behavior and drug use, and tend to have more positive life outcomes (Cohen, Fege, & Pickeral, 2009). Looking deeply into the issue of school climate in one's own school can help educators, parents, and students better understand and appreciate the often *dramatically different* school experiences that different groups of young people have inside the school on any given day.

Clearly, we know that there are subgroups of students in almost any school (highly intelligent students, struggling students, minority students, gay and lesbian students, etc.), who are socially marginalized and can routinely be targets of disrespect, bullying, or harassment by their peers. While many students might report having highly prosocial and positive school experiences every day in their school, other students may be treated in their school in ways that are simply unacceptable. These experiences steal the self-confidence, dignity, and self-respect of targeted students. Disrespectful, hurtful, and threatening school climate can rob these students of their spirit, their education, their physical and mental health, and sometimes their lives (Wessler & Preble, 2003).

It is clear from this research that the most effective schools—whether measured by academic outcomes, the promotion of democratic and civic skills, or the personal and psychological development of students—are those schools that have a safe, respectful, and personalized school climate. These are schools where students are engaged as learners, personally connected with peers and teachers, and empowered to actively apply their learning. This all occurs in ways that allow students to serve others, improve their schools and communities, and become confident and competent at solving real problems.

We refer to these schools that give focused attention to the social and emotional well-being of every child (and adult), actively value each individual in the school community, and look for ways to include all voices in the success of the school as *respectful schools*. In these schools, there is a commitment to respect throughout the school, both in and outside the classroom, for and among students as well as teachers—respect for each individual, respect for difference, and respect for the learning process.

ESSENTIAL SCHOOL CLIMATE FACTORS

There are a number of essential factors that affect school climate. First, the *relationships* that students have with their peers and adults in their school most certainly affect school climate. These relationships shape each student's perception of the school experience and provide the lens through which each student views all other activities at school. JoAnne Freiburg, an educational consultant with the Connecticut State Department of Education, has been a dedicated leader in her state's efforts to link school climate and respect to its work to improve academic outcomes for Connecticut schools. As Freiburg (2008) explains,

> School climate is very simple—it is about relationships: relationships among adults, relationships between adults and children and relationships among peers. It's about the quality of those relationships and in essence whether individuals inside schools treat each other appropriately. It boils down to this. (public presentation, March 27, 2008)

In addition to respectful relationships, we believe that respectful teaching practices are at the heart of a respectful school and shape its climate every minute of every school day. The kinds of teaching practices used at each school communicate a great deal to students about the adults' expectations, values, and beliefs. Respectful teaching practices reflect attention to the needs and interests of each child, a belief that while time or methods might need to vary for each student, learning results are achievable for every child. Respectful teaching offers students opportunities to interact with and learn from one another, foster interdependence, promote effective communication, and build rapport and respect. Respectful teaching helps create a positive school climate as it inspires students and makes them feel valued as individuals and appreciated for their ideas and contributions to the class. It makes sense that students engaged by respectful teaching practices will learn more and perform better academically. These students will feel more motivated about education in general and their school in particular, thereby perpetuating a positive school climate.

The physical environment of the school also plays an important role in school climate. A school building that is run-down, or with bathroom stalls covered in graffiti and furniture falling apart, all send a message to students about their worth and the value of their educational experience. At the same time, students who deface or disrespect their school property are communicating their own feelings for their school, adults, and their peers. Giving students responsibility to help maintain and restore their school environment is a powerful strategy for improving school climate.

Opportunities for students to participate as valued members of a school community and to feel connected to those around them contribute to a positive school climate. Nurturing a sense of belonging is also an important component of school climate. Empowering students (and teachers) to feel valued for their input into policy making, management, and improvement of the school and the surrounding community raises commitment and motivation. Promoting these positive qualities, rather than simply fighting against negative behaviors, fosters more constructive actions and continued improvement by individuals and for the school as a whole.

WE ALL WANT RESPECTFUL SCHOOLS

School climate is one of those vital but seemingly indefinable qualities that you can actually "feel" within the first few minutes you walk into a school. Each of you has spent a large portion of your life inside schools as a student, and perhaps as a teacher or administrator. You may have had communications and interactions with schools as a parent or guardian of a child. These personal experiences make you a kind of expert on school climate.

Some of you remember your former schools with fondness and others will have less positive memories. Each of the schools in your past had its own unique school climate; no two schools are exactly alike, and this is important when it comes to measuring school climate. *School climate must be assessed and addressed one school at a time.*

It is likely you remember people in your school treated you fairly or unjustly, were kind or mean, helpful, or hurtful toward you. The school was personal or impersonal for you, engaging or boring. More than likely, *certain* individuals treated you in supportive or destructive ways, *certain* teachers were respectful and engaging, while other teachers were more impersonal, rigid, or dull.

As we reflect more about our school life, we may recall more vividly the experiences we had there. We quickly recollect certain classes and certain teachers and barely remember others. We call to mind those teachers we felt were caring and genuinely interested in us and in the subjects they taught us. We may remember other teachers who were not so committed to us or to what they taught. We remember some classrooms as exciting places for learning. We may remember field trips to special places that were exciting, or ones that bored us to death. We vividly remember some things that some of our best teachers taught us years ago, as if it were yesterday. Or we draw a complete blank about years and years of instruction and recall almost nothing about what some teachers taught us.

We think about places in school that were safe and comfortable for us, and also about places that may have been scary, threatening, or even dangerous. We think about the discipline systems used in the school and their fairness and effectiveness in helping to make the school a safe and respectful place. We think about how the school or our teachers treated our parents and how closely the school interacted with our families.

We may think about student government and the students who had the chance to become leaders; we recollect those as effective, representative systems or as organizations that were closed to "unpopular" students, were elitist, or even racist. We remember the students and teachers with whom we connected on a personal level, and as much as we wish to have forgotten those who made us feel less valued and welcome, bitter memories of these interactions probably prevail.

We may still think about the so-called jocks, the nerds, the artsy kids, the theater geeks, the band and chorus kids, maybe the Goth kids, the retards, the loners, the druggies, the kids who were rumored to have committed suicide, maybe some kids who dropped out . . . but if they dropped out, you probably don't remember them at all.

When you think back on your school experiences, what do you recall that felt respectful, and what disrespectful experiences stick with you?

WHAT TEACHERS AND
STUDENTS MEAN BY RESPECT

The question of what teachers and students mean by respect was actually the starting point for a decade of school climate research we completed at Main Street Academix (MSA) (see www.msanh.com). In 1998, a new superintendent invited us as outside consultants to assist his administrative leadership team as they struggled to improve their schools. This was a district that had a reputation as a "struggling system." The district had gone through eight superintendents in eleven years, and many high school principals in the same period. Buildings, programs, budgets, and morale were in terrible shape and the taxpayers voted down the school budget every year. The drop-out rate was among the highest in the state. Families who could afford it were fleeing the system and sending their children to private schools.

One of the first things we did was meet with teachers to talk about their school's strengths and what they felt were the chief barriers to student success. On slips of paper, each teacher listed the three things that seemed the greatest impediments to their success as teachers. While there were many different "barriers" listed, only one was agreed upon by the majority of faculty—over 60 percent of the faculty mentioned "no respect here" as their primary concern.

The next day, we gathered together a highly diverse group of students from the middle and high schools. We had a very similar conversation with these students about the barriers to student success. When students were asked to write down the main obstacles they felt were getting in the way of their success, the majority of students responded, "There's just no respect around here."

At first, we were pretty amazed that both groups came up with the same problem; we thought that perhaps what the teachers wanted in their school and what the students wanted might be the same things. It also occurred to us that what the students and their teachers actually meant by the word *respect* might actually be quite different.

BEEPER STUDIES: OUR ORIGINAL
RESEARCH ON RESPECTFUL SCHOOLS

The next thing we did was to conduct research on what respect meant to students and teachers in the school. We developed an exciting and innovative research process that we designed based on the work of Csikszentmihalyi and Larson (1986) from the University of Chicago. The process we used involved the use of beepers, or electronic pagers, to randomly sample real-time respectful and disrespectful school experiences occurring at any given moment inside this school.

Here is how the beeper studies worked: First, we selected a highly diverse team of approximately thirty students and a few teachers to serve as observers inside the school. We trained these participants to conduct brief, five-minute observations when signaled by the pagers that they each kept in their pockets. We set all the pagers on vibrate and, at a specific time, we silently signaled the student and teacher researchers. The first signal told them to start paying careful attention to the *respectful* or *disrespectful* words and actions of students and teachers around them. After five minutes, we paged them all again, which indicated it was time for them to write down the examples of respect or disrespect they had observed during the past five minutes. Students and teachers carried the beepers throughout the school day, waiting for the times they would be paged to signal it was time for another observation.

Our staff at Main Street Academix and several preservice teachers at New England College purposefully selected six or eight times during each school day to silently signal the subjects. We chose times when they were in hallways passing between classes, normal class times, lunchtimes, and times before and after school.

The participants wrote down the words they heard students and teachers use, the behaviors they saw, and the responses of those who witnessed the incidents. They then labeled these situations as being either "respectful," "disrespectful," or "neither." With thirty subjects paged six to eight times a day for five days, we were able to gather over one thousand random snapshots of respectful and disrespectful interactions from each school.

As we read through the descriptions of the behaviors and words our researchers recorded during their observations, a complex and intriguing picture of respect and disrespect emerged in this school (Preble, 2003). We carefully reviewed each observation and organized the data thematically along a continuum from most disrespectful to most respectful behaviors. What was most interesting, and most troubling, was while we had plenty of examples on the disrespect side of the continuum, there were not nearly as many observations that fell on the respect side. The problem, we could plainly see, was exactly what the teachers and students identified—there really was a lot of observable disrespect happening throughout the school, but relatively few clearly described examples of respect evident in over a thousand real-time snapshots. Moreover, the behaviors that were labeled as respectful fell mostly on the lowest end of the Respect Continuum, under a heading we called *compliance*—students being "obedient" and doing what they were told—but there were not nearly so many other examples of respect recorded.

PREVENTING PITFALLS: BE AWARE OF THE TENDENCY FOR ADULTS TO DEFINE *RESPECT* AS *COMPLIANCE*

Everybody agrees that respect is important but not everyone agrees upon what respect means. Be prepared to encounter those adults who feel strongly that respect is all about student obedience and compliance. Engage in dialogue with students about what respect means to them and how this would be evident to them in school.

As we looked closer at the pile of responses labeled as being respectful, we saw that more of these had to do with what teachers were doing than with what students were doing. Our Respect Continuum that evolved from the data from the beeper study offered what became a powerful lens through which we could examine *respectful teaching and learning* practices (see Figure 1.1).

We were excited about what we had learned about respect and disrespect in schools through these beeper studies. Our challenge immediately became evident. How could we use these results to help the school develop a shared understanding of respect and disrespect at this school? How could we use these examples of respect to encourage more teachers to use respectful teaching and learning strategies as a way to improve their school?

Figure 1.1   From Violence to Empowerment: A Respect Continuum

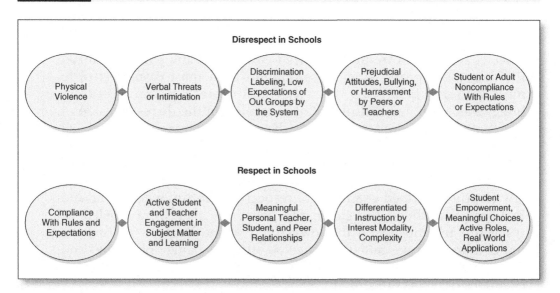

THE RESPECT CONTINUUM:
A PRACTICAL THEORY OF RESPECT

The superintendent called a meeting of his administrative team following analysis of the beeper study data and we reviewed our findings at the high school. The principals saw hundreds of examples of disrespect as well as a number of powerful forms of respect that the students and teachers had observed and recorded. Here is a brief summary of what we found in this initial beeper study research (Preble, 2003).

The Disrespect Side of the Continuum

There were very few, but some relatively serious, incidents of *violence* noted in the observers' responses. These incidences involved punching; shoving of a student, who was slightly hurt, into a locker; and one student slapping another student in the face in a hallway.

We know that schools and states have spent millions of dollars on security strategies and procedures such as safety lockdowns, metal detectors, photo IDs, locked doors, and so forth. While even one incident of school violence can change a school and community forever, there is much more to improving school climate than simply focusing on school violence.

There were a number of *threats* that students recorded. One student threatened violence toward another student, another threatened to hurt one of his peers after school. Several other students reported hearing statements that were interpreted as vague or veiled threats, but again, this was not a prevalent problem in this school.

A few students wrote about perceived issues of fairness in the form of *systemic inequities,* such as how the principal or certain teachers gave certain groups special privileges within the school, and how that angered some students. Some observers wrote about "popular students" not being punished as severely as less successful, less popular students. One observer even noted that the special education classes were all held in rooms that were more like closets than classrooms, and the fact that these rooms had no windows and poor lighting was viewed as a sign of disrespect for these students.

There was a wide range of other disrespectful occasions recorded involving students saying mean things to others. We categorized these as *verbal bullying or harassment.* Some student observers noted rather severe, even illegal, racial or sexual harassment, and a great deal of homophobic wording was recorded. Several student observers noted overhearing verbal putdowns of students with emotional, mental, or physical disabilities. Observers noted that many of these disrespectful comments were combined with taunting, name-calling, and peer rejection. Other verbal harassment was less severe, although still probably very hurtful to the targeted students—lots of comments about being a loser, a retard, fat, stupid, a fag, and so on.

There were even a few teacher comments in this set of disrespect obser-vations that seemed to reflect teachers' biased attitudes toward certain students, and that also suggested teachers may have had low expectations of these students. One student wrote, "I was heading to my fifth period class when the beeper went off. Two teachers were standing in the hallway talking. One said, 'I've got those SPED kids fifth period; they don't do anything. It's going to be a long afternoon.'" Not surprisingly, the student observer labeled this incident as disrespect.

There were also many reports of students (and teachers) *breaking school rules*, or not following teacher requests or directions in class or in the hall-ways. Classroom misbehavior included the typical and common incidents of students' chewing gum, talking while a teacher spoke, using cell phones, getting up from one's seat, and other distractions. Although these behaviors aren't threatening, they often are seen, especially by teachers, as creating a climate of disrespect.

Finding examples of disrespect was not difficult. As we mentioned, the vast majority of observations fell on the disrespect side of the continuum. While relatively few of these were physically threatening, there was a gen-eral perception, from both students and teachers, that the school was far from being a respectful place.

The Respect Side of the Continuum

As we looked at the student and teacher observations labeled as respect, an intriguing picture emerged that evolved into what is actually a rubric for respectful schools.

The majority of examples of what students called respect had to do with students simply doing what teachers told them to do in classes or hallways. We labeled this *compliance*. Anyone who has ever taught knows that without compliance, an educator cannot function or teach effectively. This process of classroom management is crucial to teacher success and the success of students.

What was also quite interesting was that a number of the comments students made about disrespect also fell into this classroom management category. For example, a student wrote, "This teacher is always yelling at us to be quiet, and then she loses it and tells a kid to shut up. That's disre-spect too." So, while compliance with a teacher's directives is necessary for teachers to do their job, the ways that teachers get their students to comply can be done either respectfully or disrespectfully. Yelling "shut up" isn't a respectful (or effective) approach to classroom management. The variety of observations in this category reflected that classrooms can be organized and orderly without being repressive.

The next set of comments related to respect from the beeper study focused on something we labeled *engagement*. Students said things like, "This teacher is respectful because she gives us stuff to do that we enjoy." Another commented, "I think it's respectful that he doesn't treat us like a bunch of sponges, just soaking up what he tells us or writes on the board." "In this class we do projects and activities that are fun." Clearly, students felt that respectful teachers did things with their students that helped them be engaged in what was happening in the class. The work in these classrooms seemed relevant to students, often involved more active learning, and had some kind of emotional resonance for students' lives. Note the shift in focus here from what students do (behaving or misbehaving) to a focus on what *the teacher* does to respectfully promote student engagement and learning.

The next set of respect observations were about *relationships.* There were many comments that noted positive, friendly, supportive, personal peer relationships happening when the beepers signaled. Also noteworthy were the comments in which students observed that they or their peers were engaged in positive relationships with their own teachers when they received the page. Students wrote: "This teacher knows all of our names . . . that's respectful." "He shows students that he cares about us doing well in his class." "I think it's respectful that this teacher takes time to talk to us about herself and the things she does outside of school and she asks us what we enjoy too . . . that's respectful." Relationships make schools more human and humane. When we see each other as "regular" people with interests and personalities that go beyond just the academic realm, students and teachers have more positive relations and work more effectively together.

An extension of the relationships theme came with a few observations that were much more specific. In these cases, students observed that they felt that it was respectful when some of their teachers "taught in different ways to different students, depending on what the students need." Or, "this teacher finds out what we are interested in and lets us do what interests us." We labeled this set of responses *personalized instruction.* "She lets us choose projects that we are interested in," said one student. "I am allowed to write my papers on the computer and that is respectful because I have trouble writing a big paper by hand without lots of mistakes." "I have finished all my work early, and she is letting me work on a new topic. I think that is more interesting than waiting around and it's respectful." When teachers modify assignments, provide choices, or allow for their students' learning differences, students identify it as respectful teaching.

Finally, our last pile of responses was unfortunately very small, but very exciting. It revealed a kind of respect that we truly believe is the key to building respectful school *empowerment.* One girl wrote,

> When the beeper went off, I had just handed in my poetry final in my English class. I thought about what was respectful and disrespectful and I thought, "this final is respectful!" Instead of making us memorize a bunch of poems or answer questions on a test, this teacher asked us to choose a genre that we really enjoyed and learned a lot about and to write our own original poem to show our understanding of that genre, then we just attached a reflection to the poem.

The next day when we beeped this girl again, she was in the same class. She wrote, "Today my teacher came into class with all of our finals (poems) bound in a leather book! She must have gone to Kinko's or someplace and she published our work in a beautiful leather book of poetry! Now, *that* is respectful!" And on the last day of our study, we happened to beep this girl again when she was involved with her English class:

> We just came back from the middle school. Our class took our book of poetry down there and had a poetry reading to the little kids in the library. When we were leaving, the middle school librarian asked us if she could borrow our book so some of the little kids could read it. She put one of those little check-out slips in the back of our book, so the middle school kids could take it home and read our poems to their families!

> Now that is empowering!

How Schools Use the Respect Continuum

After completing the beeper studies, we took what we had learned about school climate and respect and developed a student and teacher school climate survey, along with a process for implementing the surveys that involved students as researchers and leaders. We discuss this process, that we call SafeMeasures™, in much greater depth in the next several chapters.

Inviting students to be school climate researchers and to assist in implementing a schoolwide school climate survey is an empowering role. When students explain the purpose of a survey and administer it to their peers, this provides a much more effective way to collect honest and accurate survey data than when adults try to administer surveys like this on their own.

After collecting student and teacher school climate data, we shared the qualitative and quantitative data with teachers, students, and school leaders. Participants used the Respect Continuum to develop goals for improving their schools. We provided follow-up professional development for teachers to help them begin to use *respectful teaching strategies* more effectively. (For another version of the Respect Continuum, see Appendix A.)

INITIAL SUCCESS IN ONE DISTRICT

We continued to work with these schools for a number of years. The teachers began to appreciate the respect from their new superintendent, who provided them with professional development and helped them get a new contract, something that they hadn't had for years. Many of the teachers became more excited about engagement with the work to improve respect in their schools. We also established a cohort of teachers from the schools to work together to earn a master's degree that was paid for by the district. These graduate students conducted action research in their classrooms and implemented new teaching techniques while they collected data on their effectiveness. In the end, the district even got a new, state-of-the-art middle school approved and built after more than a decade of failed votes in the community. In one year, toward the end of this superintendent's tenure, 85 percent of students from the high school went on to higher education, a level unheard of before in this district.

During our research in this district, one student told us what she would do to make her school work better for all students: "Tell all the good teachers to stop leaving after a year or two to go to the richer towns." This girl felt abandoned by the system and by her teachers who chose to move on to wealthier school systems. As a result of this superintendent's leadership, a large group of caring teachers, principals, and the community stepped up to support these schools. Many good teachers chose to stay, and many of the students and families who had left the school previously decided to come back. The girl's wish was fulfilled.

This superintendent has said repeatedly that his success in turning around this struggling district began the day he announced his goal as a leader: "We may not end up being the top academic school system in the state, but we will be the kindest, most supportive, most caring and respectful district anywhere, and that will make us all more successful."

LOOKING BEYOND STOPPING MISBEHAVIOR

Striving to eliminate disrespectful behaviors is certainly a worthwhile goal for any school, but stopping disrespect is not enough. Reducing bullying and stopping fights, threats, and violence is important. But these goals of "cracking down on disrespectful student behavior" and "changing" students will not in and of themselves create a truly respectful school climate. To build a climate of respect, engagement, inspired teaching, and student empowerment, we also must encourage changes in what adults do every day in the classroom and the hallways. When we recognize the need to become respectful teachers, and learn how to more effectively support each of our students so that he or she becomes an engaged learner, we will be on our way toward building more respectful, effective schools.

Since this initial work, we have used the Respect Continuum as a guidepost for school improvement throughout the country. While we are frequently called in to help address discipline, bullying, or school safety issues, the SafeMeasures process quickly shows teachers and school leaders the need to focus more attention on *building respect*, rather than simply fighting to stamp out discipline problems or disrespect. This seems like a simple step, but moving from one side of the Respect Continuum to the other as the basis for taking corrective action makes all the difference and results in using completely different school change strategies.

PREVENTING PITFALLS: ASK TEACHERS AND ADMINISTRATORS FEARFUL OF "CHANGE" TO PERSONALIZE LEARNING AND EMPOWER STUDENTS

Prepare to address the inevitable "push back" from some educators whenever advocating for more respectful teaching practices. This can be achieved through deepening teacher-student relationships, such as initiating an advisory program or using more engaging, empowering practices such as service learning or project-based learning. It is important to have data to show such changes are necessary, as well as a clear vision for how these changes might look in your particular setting.

As teachers and students look at their school climate data, it becomes apparent that if they can develop better relations among students and teachers, make learning experiences more engaging, increase personalization, and empower students, many of the incidents of disrespect will simply disappear.

It would be naive, however, to think that a more positive climate will eliminate all issues of disrespect and assure no one ever threatens school safety. Schools still need systems of discipline, clarity of expectations, and strategies to address the most egregious behavior. But by decreasing the less extreme disrespectful behaviors, enlisting students more in contributing to the school's functioning, and reducing the frustrations of teachers being asked to continually put out small fires, everyone has a greater capacity to address the less frequent, truly dangerous threats to school safety.

We want to help schools achieve results, rather than to just say they are trying to address challenges. Research on the shortcomings of school reform shows all too well what doesn't work—top-down imposition of one-size-fits-all strategies rarely works. Many schools have tried to create more rules and escalate enforcement, yet disrespect in schools continues (and often increases).

No one solution will work for all students. Insightful work by Rob Horner and George Sugui (Office of Special Education Programs [OSEP], n.d.), who developed the Positive Behavioral Interventions and Supports (PBIS) program, advises we look at students as falling into three distinct categories. In most schools, 80 percent of students are usually responsive to any well-designed program instituted in a school—these are the "regular" kids who largely enjoy school, follow rules (most of the time), and have the foundational skills and dispositions to succeed in school. Another 15 percent of students in most schools will respond a bit differently. These students may be a bit more idiosyncratic, come from more challenging home environments, have unique learning styles, or may be going through some personal difficulties. What works for the 80 percent may not work for these students. Yet, there are actions schools can take that can work for these students; they may look different or be modified from what is being implemented for the majority. The last 5 percent is the truly needy or most at-risk group. These students may have deep-set personal difficulties, extreme circumstances outside school, or psychological profiles beyond what schools are set up to address. These students may need professional help, special contracts, or alternative programs more suited to their needs (see Figure 1.2). Making school policy based on this small minority can be oppressive for the majority and prove counterproductive. Likewise, making plans based only on the more numerous 80 percent is likely to miss a good 20 percent of the student population (OSEP, n.d.).

As we use the Respect Continuum with schools, we seek to consider related systems and strategies that are adaptable to the needs of each group of students—to not only prevent (or respond to) the worst behaviors but also to enable and encourage the best behaviors. This perspective realigns educators' roles to balance their responsibility for discipline with the fundamental goal to promote learning—*simultaneously improving both through the same process.*

School reform has all too often been an adult exercise in "changing the kids." The power of the SafeMeasures process is that it helps schools

Figure 1.2   PBIS Triangle

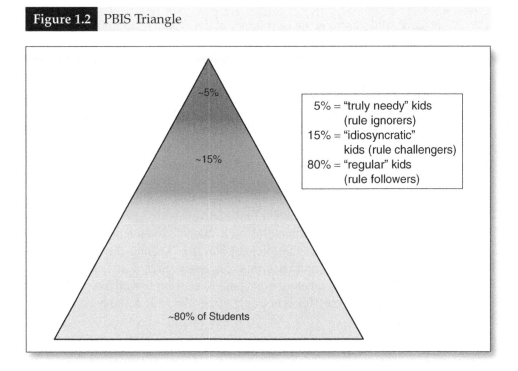

~5%

~15%

~80% of Students

5% = "truly needy" kids (rule ignorers)
15% = "idiosyncratic" kids (rule challengers)
80% = "regular" kids (rule followers)

develop the leadership potential and civic engagement of their students as partners in school reform. Students in Grades 3–12 learn to conduct research on school climate, advocate for fairness and respect for all, and expand opportunities for engaged learning and respectful teaching practices in their schools. The democratic roles that these students and their peers play embody the best of what American education should be doing—preparing its students as future citizens to stand up for what is right, to learn how to take effective action, and to provide valuable service to their communities. Incorporating adult and student leadership roles as opportunities for meaningful civic engagement is a major part of what the SafeMeasures process and this book are about.

MAKING IT REAL: A REAL-LIFE RESPECTFUL SCHOOL

Starting from scratch in 1999, Compass School was designed to be a school where every child finds success. The founders were free to build educational programs and practices closely aligned with the positive side of the Respect Continuum. It was the belief of the founding board that if students and teachers were treated with respect throughout the school program, problems would be minimized and the best in students would shine.

Students don't become angels when they walk through the Compass doors, nor is Compass free from any struggles or challenges. But what is clear, from the minute one steps into the school, is that this is a climate of respect. Even service technicians who come in the building will stop and ask, "What kind of school is this?" They invariably say something like, "I wish this kind of school was there for me when I was a kid."

What works at Compass is the consistency of the messages to students throughout the whole school program that each student is valued, there are high expectations of every child, and the school will do its utmost to assure each student can succeed in school and in life beyond school.

The expectations are that students do their best, act responsibly, follow through on commitments, and are each a contributing member of the school community. These apply whether in classes, where teachers try to personalize learning; in all-school meetings, where every Thursday ends with public "commendations" from one student or teacher to another; Project Week where every student completes an independent academic project of their own design; cleaning the building after lunch with a student advisory; student judiciary that handles most of the rare disciplinary issues following a model of restorative justice; or in any of the other diverse learning experiences required of each student. Some students take more time than others to live up to these ideals, but after hearing this message in a wealth of different settings and circumstances, every student at Compass seems to "get it" and realizes that meeting expectations, working toward a high standard of quality, and being successful is not only achievable, but actually is rewarding and gratifying.

ONE COMPASS STUDENT'S STORY

Mark came to our school having failed every class in middle school. He knew he was already labeled a "problem" child. His older sister didn't help matters much because teachers in his previous school saw her too as being rather "challenging." Mark had a shaved head, ear piercings, a few tattoos, and a troubled past. When he came to Compass, he said he wanted to have a fresh start.

Like all students at Compass, Mark was expected to set personal learning goals. The first goal he set was to be seen as a leader. (To be honest, some at the school figured simply being a high school graduate would have been enough of a stretch for Mark.) Like his peers, Mark was given choices in classes about topics to study and ways to demonstrate his learning; he often chose to use art to express his ideas, but his real talent, to our surprise, was his witty writing voice when he was able to tell stories about his life.

The small school was short on soccer players, so Mark dragged himself out on the field and proved to be the speediest runner on the team. After just a few games, he was soon admired by all for chasing down opposing forwards.

The spring play was similarly short on actors, and since the school lacked the cliques and social pressures of who or what was cool (or not), Mark figured he could audition for *Alice in Wonderland* and he brought the house down as a disheveled and distraught Humpty Dumpty.

Mark ran for student judiciary, so he could help resolve discipline issues in the school; clearly not looking like a teacher's pet, he won this position easily. He became the public spokesperson for "Jude," speaking at the weekly all-school meetings about judiciary rulings and policies. Mark emphasized that while he may not always be a role model, even he understood the importance of school rules for the good of the community.

For his senior project, Mark chose to intern with a famous glassblower, to pursue his interest in art and the possibility of a future career. And in his graduation portfolio, Mark summarized his growth at Compass, saying, "I remember now how each of the previous graduates expressed that Compass was the open door for them to find themselves. It seems by the end of our time here, we discover who we are and who we aspire to be." Mark showed us all what he was capable of becoming. What Mark achieved and managed to accomplish at Compass was exceptional by any school's standards.

CONCLUSION

With all the evidence available showing the positive effects of school climate, we are apt to think that more educational leaders and communities would be focusing on improving school climate as one of their chief priorities. But we know that addressing school climate issues and the social and emotional development of students remain secondary goals of most schools, as they continue to struggle in isolation with raising test scores and making annual yearly progress (AYP) under No Child Left Behind (NCLB). Despite concerted efforts in many schools, we are beginning to see test scores plateau, or even fall, as the solitary focus on academic performance cannot sustain the gains we hope to see.

There are many individuals and organizations stepping forward to advocate for redesigning schools using principles of respect, engagement, and personalization as their rallying cries. In the chapters that follow, we share success stories from schools across the country that hold high academic expectations for all children while also creating the conditions and supports that enable each child to reach these expectations. This book showcases schools that are effectively balancing the *desired ends with the appropriate means* to meet the academic, social, and emotional needs of their students. These models and examples and detailed descriptions of the SafeMeasures process will, we hope, provide schools and communities with the tools and resources needed to successfully balance student academic progress with improvements in school climate and respect.

BOOK STUDY QUESTIONS

1. When in a school, look around for examples of respect and disrespect—which are more common? How severe are the incidents of disrespect? How often does respect go beyond simple student compliance?

2. Think back on all of the teachers you've had in your life as a student, and then describe in a few paragraphs the qualities of your most respectful and effective teachers. What could school leaders do to bring out more of these qualities in all of the teachers or most teachers?

3. In your school experiences, how were or are students involved in any decision making related to school policy or practices?

4. In thinking about schools, where might student perspectives be helpful in figuring out how to respond to different challenges and opportunities?

5. Imagine a school characterized by some of the factors of positive school climate. How would this enhance learning and behavior and overall teacher efficacy?

2

The SafeMeasures Process

A Student-Led, Collaborative Action Research Process

Samantha Smith caught cynics unaware. She could not have been more unlike the traditional diplomats she unintentionally provoked. She made no postures. She struck no negotiating positions. She did not let the fact that she was not an expert keep her from speaking out. She refused to accept that "difficult" meant impossible. She did not believe we could afford pessimism. She set the world in a tizzy.

Gale Warner and Michael Shuman,
Citizen Diplomats (1987, p. 281)

Much of what I, Bill, have learned about the power of student leadership I learned from one of my former students, a little girl named Samantha Smith.

Before her untimely and tragic death at age 13 on August 25, 1985, Samantha Smith, a girl from a small town in Maine, taught children all over the world that they could make a big difference in the world. In her efforts to defuse the nuclear arms race, this elementary school student wrote Soviet general secretary Uri Andropov, was invited to Russia, and led cold-war superpowers to reduce their nuclear weapon stockpiles. Her life and her death in an awful plane crash, as she was returning home to begin her eighth-grade year, taught me and her classmates that we could follow in her enormous footsteps. The SafeMeasures™ process is all about Samantha's kind of student leadership—heartfelt, honest, and simple yet profound, coming from the unlikeliest of leaders. It is about providing as many students in a school as possible with a voice and the opportunity to improve the adult-ruled community in which they are required to live every day. Samantha forced adults to look in the mirror at the dangerous cold-war world they had created. SafeMeasures helps adults look afresh at their school when it comes to climate and the conditions for learning.

SARASON'S RESEARCH ON SCHOOL CHANGE

Esteemed educational researcher Seymour Sarason (1990) wrote a great book, depressingly titled *The Predictable Failure of Educational Reform*, that describes the shortcomings of American school reform efforts over time. After an exhaustive review of research on school change initiatives over a period of four decades, Sarason found that those that worked best involved some kind of "shift in power relations." Put in simple terms, when "empowering others" was a key element of the change process, then the process was much more likely to work.

Knowing that neither teachers nor administrators have time or energy to waste on predictably failing efforts, and taking Sarason's advice to heart, we designed the SafeMeasures process to bring about real change in schools. At the heart of this process lies the idea of creating "meaningful and empowering roles" (Haney, Banks, & Zimbardo, 1973) in school reform for teachers and students to build respectful and effective schools.

BALANCING ADULT AND STUDENT LEADERSHIP

All too often, well-meaning adults in schools adopt "expert" or "research-based" solutions that just plain don't work, especially when directives are top-down with no effort to shift traditional power relations. These adult-generated solutions frequently don't succeed in bringing about meaningful change. As Sarason (1990) observed, even if top-down orders in business or the military might work at times, decades of evidence show that these solutions rarely work in schools.

When these adult dominated "reforms" are repeatedly rolled out and fail to take root time and again, it is little wonder that teachers become frustrated, cynical, and even angry. How can one remain positive and eager to follow school leaders when the administrators so often make empty promises that "this time" things will improve, but continually fail to deliver much change that really affects the system in visible or meaningful ways?

When teachers see their schools continually fail to move forward in consequential and inspiring ways, they begin to feel that school change is a hopeless cause. As educators, we begin to feel we are actually helpless to change our schools. Resisting the next new idea for school change, then, actually becomes an effective survival strategy and the most rational response. Resisting change becomes a way to preserve energy and avoid raising one's hopes for real change, only to be disappointed again. When teachers resign themselves to the status quo—when they fail to see the power within themselves, their colleagues, or their leaders to make a difference in the lives of their students or the life of their school—this becomes a prescription for learned helplessness. This is the great killer of teacher excellence and passion. To battle these debilitating conditions within teachers and schools, we use *collaborative action research*, a process that brings students to the table with new kinds of data to help teachers improve their schools.

PREVENTING PITFALLS: ALLOW STUDENTS TO HELP ADULTS SUSTAIN SCHOOL IMPROVEMENT EFFORTS

What we have seen for many years is that teachers and administrators get more deeply invested in school improvement work when they have students working directly with them as partners. While adults can be difficult with one another at times, these same adults are usually, in our experience, "better behaved" in the company of their students—more focused, more positive, and more open to listening to a variety of ideas. Teachers frequently tell us they enjoy working with students as partners in school reform projects. They feel it is more engaging when students are involved. We like to say that students can bring out the best in teachers and administrators.

A recent report by Clemson University's National Dropout Prevention Center on one of our collaborative dropout prevention projects emphasized the importance of including student leaders as partners in dropout prevention as an "exemplary practice." In schools where adults worked in partnership with student leadership teams, evaluators from the National Dropout Prevention Center found higher levels of implementation of the dropout prevention plans and enhanced "fidelity of implementation" and sustainability of the intervention. These findings provide further justification for school leaders to invite students to the table as partners in school improvement.

Source: Hammond, Linton, Smink, & Drew, 2007.

THE SAFEMEASURES PROCESS: AN OVERVIEW

The SafeMeasures collaborative action research process is not rocket science. It is really just a commonsense, thoughtfully designed process for systemically working to improve schools. What is unusual about SafeMeasures is not its steps—countless organizational change programs offer a similar list. What is unique, we find, is how uncommon such a thorough, data-driven, student-centered, sustainable process is for schools. For a variety of reasons—such as time constraints, hierarchies, traditions, existing power relations, and limited vision—schools often address issues in a piecemeal fashion, jump to solutions without clearly identifying the problem, and impose adult responses with little understanding of students' perspectives.

SafeMeasures seeks to provide a logical process to build school capacity for continual improvement in climate and learning. It is based on research and experience on school change, emphasizing the value of collaborative action research to bring together those most directly involved in a school to impact the quality of learning for each member of the school community.

SafeMeasures is characterized by five key elements:

1. Inclusion of students and teachers as leaders throughout the process

2. Collection of site-specific data from all students and teachers in that school setting

3. Analysis of data by students and teachers to identify issues and subsequently set goals and benchmarks for improvement

4. Action project planning and implementation directly tied to these goals

5. Ongoing data collection to monitor progress, adjust action, and sustain change for continuous school improvement

Stage One of the process establishes the overall design of the process. This requires initial contact with the school administration to learn about school goals and to ensure administrative support for the process. Particularly important at this initial stage is assuring that formal school leaders are truly open to feedback from teachers and students, and willing to include both of these essential groups in the change process. Without this support, we know from experience, as well as Sarason's (1990) admonition, our work will not do much to change climate or learning in the school. Thus, the adult design team (DT) is put together and a diverse student leadership team (SLT) is selected.

Stage Two involves collecting data on a wide range of school issues from all students and teachers. This is done through surveys and focus groups, collecting both qualitative and quantitative data. Students lead in this data collection process, sending a visible message to their peers that every voice is valued. This process is clearly different from adult run processes more typical in most schools.

Stage Three brings teachers and students together to look at their school's data. Reviewing statistical summaries and selections of quotes from open-ended questions, students and teachers set goals related to each of the National School Climate Standards (see pages 50–51) and tie these goals directly to their data. A voting process involving members of the student leadership team and all faculty allows prioritization of goals to focus on a few that seem most ripe for change.

Stage Four is the exciting phase of planning action projects and beginning their implementation. We try to encourage groups to get to this stage as quickly as they can, avoiding talking ideas into the ground and looking for the "perfect" solution. In practice, we have never seen one action project that can solve a problem for all—instead, we push groups to undertake several projects to address their goal, knowing that sometimes just taking any action can send a powerful message of change to those in school. Change is messy and complex; student and teacher leaders build skill and capacity to change by undertaking projects, adjusting based on experience, and continually looking for ways to achieve goals despite inevitable stumbles and setbacks.

Stage Five focuses on sustainability of the school change process. SafeMeasures is not a one shot program but a process for ongoing, continuous organizational improvement. At its core, it is about developing leadership teams, collecting and analyzing data to set goals, using these goals to generate action projects, then building on successes (and failures) to work toward ever more ambitious goals. Stage Five directs leaders to collect new data to reflect on their progress, adjust their plans based on what they have learned, set new goals for themselves and their school, and renew the process for taking action based on these new goals.

While the action research process is fairly commonly used (Sagor, 2000, 2005), we know that involving students as research, design, and action partners is not nearly so common in most schools. By making teachers *and* students central to the SafeMeasures process, not only do schools gain the perspectives of the "resident experts" inside the school, but they enlist these key stakeholders in the change process, and thereby dramatically increase the likelihood of success.

BANDURA'S RESEARCH ON SELF-EFFICACY

One of the primary goals of our work and of collaborative action research itself is to help participants, both students and adults, learn how to effectively solve important school problems that affect climate and learning. Evidence suggests that a school climate with open, healthy, and collegial professional interactions, along with strong academic emphasis, empowers teachers and creates norms of collective efficacy. These conditions shape the normative environment of schools and influence teacher behavior (Bandura, 1986, 1997). Schools can intentionally cultivate this sense of efficacy—the belief that one's actions make a difference:

> When teachers believe that they can organize and execute their teaching in ways that are successful in helping students learn, and when the school climate supports them, teachers plan more, accept personal responsibility for student performance, are not deterred by temporary setbacks, and act purposefully to enhance student learning. It is important to try to understand how specific school climate attributes influence critical teacher behaviors that improve teaching and learning in the classroom. (StateUniversity .com, n.d., para. 9)

This passage captures the primary goal of a student-led, collaborative action research process, suggesting the need to help build *personal efficacy* in students and teachers as a way to improve schools. We focus on personal efficacy because we know that people who believe that they have the power to affect change, whether it be change in themselves and their own lives, change in their school, change in their community, or change in the world, will challenge themselves to try new ideas and practices, and do whatever it takes to succeed without giving up when the going gets tough.

Collaborative action research is a key tool for school improvement because it has been shown that this approach can improve teacher efficacy (Tschannen-Moran, Woolfolk Hoy, & Hoy, 1998). It is when teachers work along with colleagues—looking at data from their own school, clearly identifying a problem, designing and implementing a project to improve the situation, and collecting new data that show the change has actually worked—that teachers build effectiveness and sense of personal and professional efficacy.

We include the empowerment of students as part of our model for school reform because we know that every successful student needs to believe in his or her own talents and ability to succeed. But it is also essential in a democratic society that our educational system produces young citizens who are civically skilled; they understand how they can actively advocate for changes and initiate action that has the potential to impact the civic life of their community (Cohen, Fege, & Pickeral, 2009).

When teachers and students engage together in collaborative action research as a tool for school improvement, they develop shared understandings and interests that alter the dynamics of relationships in schools.

When teachers and students work side by side, examining data and discussing their meaning, they each begin to see issues in new ways as they appreciate the perspectives of others.

When teachers and students set goals for change and work together to design projects to address these problems, they feel a sense of ownership and pride in the success of the initiative and its results. They are more likely to work harder to make their projects succeed than they would if someone else imposed the work upon them.

When data collected during and after implementation of a project show evidence that changes have actually occurred, the group celebrates their success. Their belief in their ability to do this work successfully again is strengthened. The teacher or student leader comes to believe, "The things I do can really matter and make a difference"—this is the meaning of efficacy.

LOOKING DEEPLY AT COLLABORATIVE ACTION RESEARCH

Kurt Lewin is credited with the creation of action research in the 1940s. However, the nature of action research has changed significantly ever since. There are many effective "action research" models for improving schools and school climate, reducing bullying, and increasing school safety (Cohen, Fege, & Pickeral, 2009; Farrington & Ttofi, 2009; Olweus, 1972, 1993; Preble & Taylor, 2008; Sagor, 2000, 2005). Each of these can serve as a roadmap for working on school climate.

More than a decade of experience doing this work in schools has convinced us that bringing together a diverse, broadly representative adult school climate improvement team—made up of school administrators, teachers, and often parents and community members—is an essential first step in improving school climate. Involving the principal is critical because of the influence a principal can have on the organization and priorities of a school. Incorporating teachers, especially those most respected by their colleagues within the building, is also significant. Teachers' voices must be heard as part of the process of school improvement, because ultimately it is the work that teachers do that has the most powerful effect on school climate. The roles and responsibility of the adult design team are detailed in the next chapter.

The picture changes dramatically, however, when a school chooses to also include the "true experts" on school climate and learning within any school—a diverse, representative team of students—in the process of school reform and redesign. School climate is something with which students are intimately familiar, and every student experiences the climate in the school from a unique perspective. Students involved in special education see their school in ways that are very different from regular education students. Minority students often have different school experiences from students who are members of the racial majority. Some of the most striking differences in student perceptions relating to school climate can be found in almost any school when we compare college bound and noncollege bound students. Involving these different types of students as local experts on school climate as members of a student leadership team can make all the difference when it comes to the effectiveness of the school climate improvement process. A recent study of successful school change completed by the National Dropout Prevention Center emphasized that involving students as partners was the crucial force for assessing, improving, and sustaining school climate improvement (as cited in Hammond, Linton, Smink, & Drew, 2007).

We believe that the best way to understand and improve schools is to work closely with the school's administration, teachers, and students to collect valid, reliable data on both student academic performance and school climate. These results are then used to promote professional and personal reflection, dialogue, and collaborative action (DuFour, DuFour, Eaker, & Many, 2006; Fullan, 1993, 2001, 2008). We have seen this process work effectively to improve school climate, safety, respect, and learning in hundreds of schools throughout the nation. When administrators, teachers, *and* students work together, this deep, open, honest collaboration immediately begins to improve relationships and the climate of trust within a school. These enhanced relationships help build capacity in the school to solve problems in the short-term, and if supported and sustained, they can become a powerful tool for school improvement over time.

The ultimate goal of a school climate improvement team is to build positive, respectful relationships within the school and to improve conditions for learning and the social-emotional development of students. Collaborative action research is an opportunity for diverse teams of students and adults to work together in a highly visible way, to ask questions and seek answers that will affect change for the good of their school and those within it. This process of teachers and students working together on school improvement actually models the kind of positive school climate and respectful relationships that the team aims to achieve at the broader school and community level.

EMANCIPATORY RESEARCH

Another interesting and perhaps more provocative way to view the SafeMeasures process is through the lens of emancipatory research (Baker & Lynch, 1999). "Emancipatory research can be used to 'bring voice' to excluded and marginalized groups as subjects rather than objects of research, and which attempts to understand the world in order to change it" (Lather, 1991). While this view of research is most often associated with feminist, disability rights, and antiracist approaches to research, it is equally applicable to students and teachers who instead of being seen as powerful partners for school reform, too often might be viewed as part of the problem.

When a school intentionally expands membership of its student leadership team beyond the typical academically or socially successful students, and includes targeted students or members of out-groups, this sends a message that the school "gets it." These less traditional leaders often have firsthand experience with bullying, violence, discrimination, the school's discipline systems, school failure, or hateful behavior at school. By reaching out to students who may fall outside the normal range of traditional leaders, the school's administration and teachers convey a desire to understand their school in new ways, and help *all* students succeed and have a voice in finding new ways to move the school forward.

Using student empowerment as a school improvement strategy is consistent with the practice of collaborative, participatory, and emancipatory action research. At the very center of the SafeMeasures process, we try to impress upon schools the opportunity they can offer students who may be routinely exposed to ridicule, threats, or social isolation. The school can provide these students with the power to educate others about themselves, along with what works for them and what doesn't. We show educators how these opportunities for leadership can bring purpose and hope back into these students' lives and, at the same time, provide educators with powerful insights about their schools. Including these students in school improvement can transform negative energy into positive, proactive civic engagement to be part of the solution rather than part of the problem.

PREVENTING PITFALLS: INCLUDE STUDENT VOICE WITHOUT REDUCING TEACHER POWER

Collaborative action research is not about blame or who gets credit but about working together for overall improvement on the targeted issue. Data gathered are meant to offer formative snapshots (as opposed to summative judgments) of a school's strengths and needs that can serve to guide decisions, plans, and action. Including students brings expert knowledge on life in schools and how to effect change. The research process can frame "problems" as an expected feature of schools and as opportunities for problem solving, collaboration, innovation, and leadership.

MAKING IT REAL: SCHOOL CLIMATE IMPROVEMENT

When slapped with a consent decree from the U.S. Department of Justice for failures to effectively address peer-on-peer racial harassment and discrimination, in Tennessee, Sullivan County Director of Schools John O'Dell was compelled to act. He invited Main Street Academix (MSA) to help effect change in school climate from within the system. O'Dell had begun his career as an administrator believing he would call the shots, but now, near retirement in an ever more complicated world, he realized his ability to individually address increased demands was all too limited.

In their initial contact, consultants from MSA laid out the process and the requirement of putting students and teachers at the center of the work. Students from all social, academic, and racial groups were enlisted to join student leadership teams in each of the district's schools. These students were interviewed so that they could share their perspectives on the problems they saw every day in their schools—problems that the adults had clearly misunderstood. The students were trained to facilitate data collection on school climate, and they encouraged their peers to take their work to improve school safety, climate, and respect for all students seriously. The students worked with their teachers to develop data-driven action plans and projects, and continually assessed their progress toward improving school climate.

Students and their teachers used the SafeMeasures process to address the difficult problem of racial bias and discrimination in their schools, as well as the broader problems of school climate, respect, student engagement in learning, and adult effectiveness in dealing with challenging discipline issues. Even though the work of the student leadership teams initially focused on addressing the racial harassment complaints, the district continued with the SafeMeasures process to improve school climate, student engagement, and learning because they saw it was working. Sullivan County established a systemwide student leadership initiative that they called their Respect and Leadership (R & L) Teams. The initiative is still in place today, nearly nine years after it began in response to the Justice Department's consent decree.

In one of the toughest of the five regional high schools in the district, the initial data they received highlighted no shortage of problems—disrespect between students, unresponsive teaching, uneven discipline practices, unclean halls, fearfulness at using the bathrooms, intimidation in the parking lot. These were deflating, although not surprising, results, and very overwhelming.

Small groups from the student and adult leadership teams created goals related to their analysis of the data, and these were posted around the room on big sheets of paper. When it came time to vote on goal priorities, most shied away from the most challenging areas (who was ready to take on years of entrenched teaching practices?), but the areas of school cleanliness, better parking lot safety, and usable bathrooms (who can learn if waiting until they get home to go to the bathroom?) seemed a reasonable start for these student and teacher leaders.

Action plans led to the vibrant new principal being out in the parking lot every morning, rain or shine, to greet students (and monitor behavior); teachers more present in the halls during passing periods, along with student hall monitors; respect bracelets distributed by student leadership team members; student decorated bathrooms; some schoolwide assemblies on respect along with discussions in advisory; and student and teacher recognition of positive behaviors by "catching" random acts of kindness.

One year later, behavioral problems were down, students felt safe using the bathrooms, hallways had been painted, and the parking lot was safer and more orderly. Were the adult and student leadership teams finished? They were not, but what a solid start—now on to the tougher, but potentially even more potent issues around teaching and learning.

On several occasions, Sullivan County's R & L Teams have made in-person and Skype presentations about their work at statewide, regional, and national conferences. In those Sullivan County schools that significantly improved school climate, like this roughest of high schools, not only are there fewer discipline problems, but academic performance is up considerably as well. Sullivan County is doing a great deal to enlarge the voices of students and to find new ways to allow students to help adults keep their "finger on the pulse" of their school and get school improvement right.

CONCLUSION

The SafeMeasures process was developed based on what is known about the unfortunately rare instances of effective school reform. Sarason's research instructs us to make sure that we approach change in schools by challenging and altering existing power relations, including students and teachers who will ultimately choose to either support or undermine the change process.

Action research is a process of grass-roots inquiry that empowers the researcher as an active agent of change. When teachers and student leaders collect data and begin to see that their efforts are resulting in successful, measurable change, it gives them hope and a sense of renewed self-belief in their own abilities to make a difference.

Working as a school community using collaborative action research can promote a sense of personal and professional effectiveness and provide momentum for meaningful, sustainable, locally led school reform.

BOOK STUDY QUESTIONS

1. How does change occur in your school? Who leads it? Who makes the decisions? Who implements change? How effective is the process of change in reaching goals?

2. What steps of the SafeMeasures change process does your school use already (overall planning, data collection, data analysis and goal

setting, action planning and implementation, sustainability)? Which are most uncommon at your school?

3. We know that your school collects loads of data. How do teachers and administrators currently use these data? What kinds of data does your school have on school climate? What other school climate data could you collect to provide a more balanced perspective on how your school is working?

4. If students were more frequently involved in the change process in the school, how do you think the process and results would differ? What could you gain by including the perspectives, ideas, and energy of students?

5. Students as partners: Think of the term *student leader* and the kinds of students that fit this description at your school. Now think of the word *expert* and think of students who may be experts or who have intimate knowledge, skills, or experience with issues or problems that you or other adults may not fully understand (such as how to set the clock on the DVD). How could you invite these experts to help make your school a better place?

3

Stage One: Everyone Is a Leader

Empowering Students and Teachers

The failure of educational reform derives from a most superficial conception of how "complicated settings" like schools are organized: their structure, their dynamics, their power relationships, and their underlying values and axioms. . . . Schools will remain intractable to desired reform as long as we avoid confronting (among other things) their existing power relationships . . . avoiding those relationships is precisely what educational reformers have done, thus ensuring that the more things change, the more they remain the same.

Seymour Sarason, *The Predicable Failure of Educational Reform* (1990, pp. 4–5)

Stage One of the SafeMeasures™ process begins by assembling two strategically designed leadership teams who will work together to lead and support school climate improvement and change. The adult design team (DT) is made up of a representative group of teachers, administrators, and student support personnel who are tied to as many parts of the "system" as possible. Rather than adding one or two "student leaders" to this team, we advocate for the school to develop a parallel, broadly representative team of student leaders to form a student leadership team (SLT). It takes a special kind of principal to assemble and work collaboratively with these teams to share what are often viewed as the administrator's roles and responsibilities for school leadership.

THE DIGNITY OF EXPERTISE

What is it about being invited to the table of power, where decisions are being debated, shaped, and made, that is so inspiring to a person? In my first year as a new teacher, I, Bill, was so honored when my principal invited me to become one of the twenty-two members of our school's "decision team." I honestly believe that being allowed to take on this empowering role as a brand new, wet-behind-the-ears teacher transformed me as an educator and made me become an advocate for school change.

This decision team was the place where things happened in my school. The invitation to serve on this team made me feel like an adult (I was twenty-three) and a professional. It taught me how complex our school was pedagogically, politically, professionally, and economically. I felt a new kind of responsibility to question what was working and not working in our school, and to do more than simply complain about things that I felt needed to be improved. I learned that a true professional has both the responsibility and the opportunity to help improve education.

The longer I served as a member of our decision team, I actually began to feel like something of a school expert and an educational leader. I know I am not the only one to be affected by the power of being invited to the table as a leader. One of the most compelling lessons we have learned in our twenty-five years of empowering students and teachers is the simple yet transformative power of picking students (and teachers) to be leaders.

Bill Cumming (2008), the founder of the Boothby Institute, has spoken eloquently about what he calls "the dignity of expertise." This is the notion that every student is an expert on his or her own school experiences; every teacher is an expert on the things that work and do not work in his or her classroom or school. The dignity of expertise offers a powerful rationale for bringing diverse groups of teachers and students together as leaders and honoring the unique and invaluable viewpoints they each bring to the team. These teams can provide insights and input that shed light on a school's assets and weaknesses in ways that no single "expert" can.

GETTING STARTED

As educational reformers, we can begin to address Sarason's warning about the "predictable failure" of school reform efforts by agreeing that we will not underestimate how complicated schools really are as organizations.

At every turn, we must consider ways to address and challenge existing power relationships within the system. We must continually ask ourselves, what is fundamentally different about the ways we are doing business this time? How are the roles we create going to be different? How is our decision-making process different? How is the membership of leadership groups more inclusive?

As we plan for improving schools, let's begin by agreeing that no two schools are truly alike. No group of students shares the same needs, talents, or interests. No group of teachers responds to feedback or calls for change in quite the same way, and there are no "magic bullets" when it comes to improving our schools in meaningful ways. We know from experience, there is no individual program, model, theory, strategy, or simple solution that we can count on to work for every school, every student, or every teacher. While solutions to a school's problems should be informed by solid educational theory and valid research on best practices, in the end, local school leaders must frame, adapt, and customize these solutions. Approaches to school problems must fit the unique profile of each school. It takes local knowledge of the adult, student, and community culture to make these critical decisions and to champion and guide implementation of a change process within any school.

Next, we must ask who will be the "school reformers"? If we listen carefully to Sarason, we can predict who will typically be appointed to direct the reform—principals, superintendents, central office personnel, school boards, elected officials, special interest professionals, or elite parents. These are highly educated, connected, well-spoken (in English) people with political, social, or economic power. Teachers are often added to this list of school reformers, but in many schools, their influence is limited. Students are almost never invited.

If students are invited to participate in school reform discussions, we can predict which students will be at the table—school-smart, successful students—whom many teachers call their "natural leaders." Of all the challenges we face as SafeMeasures consultants, the debate over which students should be included as school improvement partners is the first and most important challenge. We work hard to show school leaders that if they want to heed Sarason's warning about predictable failure and address power relations differently, they must invite at least some "unnatural" leaders to the table.

Who might these atypical leaders be? They are those less academically successful, less popular, maybe even less physically attractive, or less verbally adept students who so often get passed over as school leaders. Who would be more eminently qualified to design, lead, and advocate for specific changes within a school to improve school climate, respect, and learning for *every* student than students who live and breathe the wide variety of experiences that occur every day within their schools? When adults seek out and invite those who represent the diversity of their community to be its leaders—those students who thrive as well as those who struggle socially, emotionally, academically, and behaviorally—they show they understand the unique forms of expertise that each of these students brings to the table. Inviting those students who may seem most unlikely leaders can transform these students' self-perceptions as well as the kind of people they ultimately become.

AN UNLIKELY LEADER

I, Bill, remember this really big kid named Hank, a sophomore at a New Hampshire high school who wore a black leather jacket at all times and was clearly part of the tough crowd at his school. Hank's teachers had invited him to be a member of the student leadership team to help improve the school. He had managed to get his permission slip turned in and came with several of his peers to the first meeting.

We were sitting in chairs in a large circle of about eighteen people in the library. As the meeting began, two of Hank's friends who had also been invited started getting loud and fooling around. Hank quietly told them to "shut up and listen." They ignored him, and also the facilitator who was there to work with the students. After Hank interrupted the meeting a few times to admonish these two boys, who clearly were not interested in this role, the boys started teasing Hank, calling him "Mr. Big Shot" and "the big leader." Hank stood up, towering over the two boys, and said loudly, "Why don't you two shut up and listen? If they are going to treat me like a leader, then I am going to act like a leader. Now shut the heck up!" The two boys left, but Hank stayed and flourished as a school change partner.

Hank remained part of his school's student leadership for the next three years as an active, engaged member of the team. He often spoke up for those students in the school whom some teachers had written off as "losers" and had given up on. Hank was able to show his peers and teachers that students like him had much to offer and he brought real "street cred" to the leadership team over the years of his service to that school.

PREVENTING PITFALLS: INVITE DIVERSE STUDENT LEADERS

One effective strategy we have used to try to prevent adverse teacher reactions to the selection of nontraditional leaders is to ask the teachers to write a brief story about a time they remember being "picked" by an adult for something important. They write powerful stories about their own life-changing moments when they were selected to become a member of a sports team, a play, a school band, or even to be the line leader for a day. This exercise reminds teachers of the power they have to use "picking students" as a strategy that can transform a student's life. After this exercise, teachers are more likely to select a wide range of students to play important roles as members of their school's student leadership team. At this point, we ask them to submit names of students they believe may contribute important new perspectives to help the SLT better understand and address school climate issues.

ADMINISTRATIVE SUPPORT IS ESSENTIAL

What we are talking about here is empowering both teachers and students as a starting point for changing our schools. As anyone who has spent any time in schools or other hierarchically organized bureaucracies knows, decisions to allow empowerment of those with less authority come from the top—the principal, superintendent, department head, or other formal leader. Empowering others in most schools is at best an option of "power allotment" by those already in power. No wonder Sarason found that shifting power relations is most central for changing schools, yet so difficult to achieve. It takes a forward-looking leader to have the self-confidence to empower others and then to guide them in ways that are responsive and effective.

To be frank, we do not expect schools to soon become wholly democratic organizations run by students, teachers, and parents. There are legitimate reasons and responsibilities that should remain the purview of formal leaders. The best hope for effective reform in schools, though, lies with those formal leaders (including teachers) who listen; seek the input of others in the design of school policies, programs, and practices; and make decisions openly and as democratically as possible. Administrative support for participatory leadership and governance, we believe, is at the heart of a respectful and effective school that is deliberately moving forward. Missing this "empowerment reality check" on the principal's leadership and willingness to listen to the ideas, opinions, and feedback of teachers and students can have unfortunate and profoundly negative effects.

PREVENTING PITFALLS: SECURE ADMINISTRATIVE SUPPORT

Over the past decade, we have learned about the importance of administrative support the hard way. There have been times when a teacher, parent, or school representative managed to begin the SafeMeasures process without sufficient principal knowledge, understanding, and support. These adults assembled a student leadership team with the best of intentions. They collected school climate data and developed action plans that, when they came to the attention of the principal, were eventually ignored, scoffed at, and rejected out of hand.

Students were devastated. After all of their optimism, their pride in being selected as school leaders, their supposed empowerment, and the hope they had for a brighter and more promising future for their school, they were summarily put back in their boxes, silenced, and made powerless by a principal who did not believe in student voice and empowerment. Imagine the message about power that this experience sent to these student leaders.

In-depth meetings with a school's administrative team begin the SafeMeasures process. The initial meeting involves listening to the administrators' perspectives and vision, learning about the school's unique culture and needs, and discovering what the formal leaders hope to achieve. We draw attention to how to best accomplish results, emphasizing the inherent power teachers and students have to undermine or facilitate the change process. We also emphasize the importance of using school climate work to align the plethora of initiatives already going on in a school. If principals are ready to focus on results and build capacity for sustained school improvement, willing to share leadership, and open to different approaches to all too familiar challenges, we are ready to begin the real work of school change.

THE ADULT DESIGN
TEAM: MEMBERSHIP AND ROLES

After assuring the support of the school's administration, the next step is to have the principal bring together an adult design team (DT) of committed—and possibly even some skeptical—but reasonably open-minded adults to work collaboratively to plan for the school climate improvement process. One of the main factors that determine the overall success of any intervention in a school is the level of buy-in from teachers, but also from students and parents as well. If you are an educator who has worked inside a school for more than a few years, think about how many school reform initiatives you have seen fail because teachers or students either passively or aggressively resisted the change. The challenge in working on school climate is to design and help implement a process that can overcome this resistance to change.

After the principal has invited anywhere from three to fifteen teachers, guidance counselors, nurses, special educators, teacher's aides, coaches, and possibly parent representatives to become the school's adult DT, the collaborative work begins. The team needs to determine its mission and the purpose of its existence, and establish norms such as the ways meetings will be run, who will take notes, facilitate, and keep the team on track.

To prepare our adult DTs for their roles as school climate leaders, we showcase the importance of school climate, safety, and respect in schools. We share important research (Cohen & Elias, 2010; Preble & Taylor, 2008; U.S. Department of Health and Human Services, 2001; U.S. Secret Service, 2002) showing that a safe and respectful learning environment is one of the most important things a school can provide. This is what ensures every student the opportunity to learn and to develop into a healthy, socially, and emotionally well-adjusted person.

We next review the Respect Continuum, discussed in Chapter 1, to frame the kinds of action steps, programs, and practices that work to improve school climate and respect in a school. We share specific stories about how schools around the country are successfully and passionately doing this important work. The team learns that students who are frightened at school, bullied on the bus, bored in class, disconnected from adults, and disengaged in the classroom will not learn anywhere near as well as they would if the social, emotional, and academic climate within the school were better. This is the real charge of the adult design team—to better understand and improve school climate and learning so that all students have an opportunity to reach their full potential.

Adults on the DT come to quickly see that even among team members, perceptions about climate at the school may vary widely. Some teachers may feel that "everything is just fine" in their school. Other teachers express worry about bullying of certain subgroups or individuals within the school. Still others cite statistics on the number of dropouts, numbers of behavior problems at school, fights, and suspensions. Others bemoan the high numbers of disengaged students in their classes who seem to have given up or do not seem to care about school or learning.

It is not a big leap for this group to quickly see the connection between school climate and student learning and the challenges we face in these areas today. The group soon understands that if schools are expected to do an increasingly better job ensuring that each student demonstrates higher order thinking, personal growth, and academic achievement, then school climate must be part of the solution. The team understands that if incidents of rule breaking, social and emotional problems, and academic failure are on the rise, then one of the most logical and powerful interventions educators can make is a concerted effort to positively impact the climate of their school. If they are expected to ensure that all children learn at increasingly higher levels, then the quality of interpersonal relationships must be strong for each student. If more is expected of their school, then the engagement and motivation of students in learning, the rigor and relevance of the curriculum, and the connectedness of everyone within the school must be considered to attain these improvements.

One very important realization that our adult DT comes to understand is that the work of improving school climate and learning is not an add-on. It is not just another so-called initiative to layer on top of all the other initiatives smothering our schools these days. Improving school climate and learning is a big idea, not a program. It represents an understanding of the connectedness of all aspects of the educational system. How can teacher-student relationships, student engagement and motivation, and peer respect and belonging be separated from the rest of what goes on inside schools every day? Quite simply, it can't.

**PREVENTING PITFALLS: ACKNOWLEDGE
THAT ADULTS WILL HAVE DIFFICULTY FINDING
TIME OR COMMITTING TO THEIR LEADERSHIP ROLES**

Time is always a big challenge for sustaining the commitment of adults to school initiatives. We have found that when the superintendent, school board, and principal all articulate publically the importance of school climate for improving safety and learning in schools, then support and resources like time tend to grow. When teachers on the design team understand that this is a systemic effort, they take it more seriously. When the school provides design team members with time to support their work through professional learning communities, this makes the effort even more sustainable.

NATIONAL SCHOOL CLIMATE STANDARDS AS A GUIDE TO ACTION

One of the problems with school climate is how fuzzy the idea seems when we try to define and ultimately measure or assess it. At MSA, we have used our own school climate research and the research of many others to help school administrators and adult design team members better understand and improve school climate. We developed our original school climate surveys and interventions based on school climate factors we originally discovered through our beeper study research with students and teachers (Preble, 2003). These elements of school safety, peer respect and belonging, and student-teacher relationships became the foundation for our Respect Continuum. The continuum provides a roadmap for moving from just reducing negative behaviors to cultivating a positive climate of respect and engagement for all.

In 2009, the National School Climate Council developed a set of National School Climate Standards to more fully and clearly define the issue of school climate. These standards are a wonderful tool for focusing school climate leadership training and school-level data collection and action planning. For our purposes, we use a summary of these standards when training adult design teams.

ABBREVIATED NATIONAL SCHOOL CLIMATE STANDARDS

Bill Preble and his colleagues from Main Street Academix developed this abridged version of the National School Climate Standards to simplify previous versions and to make the standards easier to use for school climate improvement dialogue, education, and leadership.

- Standard 1: Develop a *vision and plan of action* to improve school climate, based on school climate data and input from all stakeholders including teachers, parents, administrators, community partners, and students.
- Standard 2: Develop *specific policies and systems of support* to promote student engagement in academic, social, emotional, ethical, and civic learning and to support the reengagement of disengaged students in school.
- Standard 3: Identify and support *teaching practices and learning opportunities* to promote positive social, emotional, ethical, and civic learning, as well as rigorous academic learning. Develop infrastructure, programs, and systems to support engaged learning and respectful, effective teaching.
- Standard 4: Develop a *safe, welcoming environment* where all members of the school community feel safe, respected, and supported—socially, emotionally, physically, and intellectually.
- Standard 5: Create meaningful opportunities for students to *learn and practice civic responsibility*, be committed to *social justice*, and develop the skills and values that are essential in a democratic society.

This document was adapted from the National School Climate Council's *National School Climate Standards: Benchmarks to promote effective teaching, learning and comprehensive school improvement* (2009), developed by Jonathan Cohen and Terry Pickeral. (For a detailed description of the National School Climate Standards, visit www.schoolclimate.org/climate/documents/school-climate-standards-csee.pdf.)

The National School Climate Standards serve as a clear and comprehensive guide to embrace the whole gamut of issues alongside the "safe and welcoming environment" aspects of school climate that most typically come to mind when educators begin to consider improving climate. These new standards emphasize school policies, infrastructure and systems of support, teaching and learning practices, and student civic engagement and empowerment to address issues of social justice in schools. For an adult leadership team, these standards offer a broad operational framework to serve as a guide for the team's purpose and mission.

The standards also drive home the importance of viewing school climate from a systemic perspective rather than narrowly focusing exclusively on school violence or bullying prevention. Given this broader purview, a key factor in assembling an effective adult DT is to include teachers who are members of other major school improvement initiatives currently underway related to issues covered by the National School Climate Standards. For example, if your school presently has a school improvement committee, positive behavior and supports team, technology committee, discipline committee, assessment committee, or student advisory committee, then members of these committees (who may be working relatively independently and maybe even at cross purposes from each other) should be invited to become members of the adult DT. Bringing issues of school climate and learning back to their existing committees, then, also becomes their job. In this way, each initiative does not become simply another add-on in the school. Just as school climate is a "whole child" initiative, so is it a "whole school" initiative.

These are tall orders for any school. The teachers and school leaders who work together soon realize that they cannot do this work alone. They may quickly recognize that their students are actually the real experts on many of these issues. Furthermore, providing students with the opportunity to work with adults on these school climate issues actually begins to address National School Climate Standard 5—civic engagement and social justice. The next step, then, is to develop a robust, diverse student leadership team to serve as leadership partners.

SELECTING A DIVERSE TEAM OF STUDENT LEADERS

To broaden the sphere of its expertise and influence, the adult design team recruits a student leadership team to work alongside them in improving school climate and learning. The opportunity to serve as local experts on the climate and effectiveness of their school is an exciting and empowering experience for these students.

THE PRIDE OF BEING PICKED

As Manny, a high school student we recently worked with, told us, "I couldn't believe they picked me to be on the leadership team. My mother didn't believe me for a while either!" Manny's teacher said, "I chose him because he really needs things like this in his life. He is practically raising himself, is having some real problems in school, and all he has talked about this week is being picked to be a leader." Manny did a remarkable job collecting data from his peers, emphasizing the value of their perspectives. Seen in this role by his peers and teachers, he led the student leadership team in the task of rewriting the discipline handbook to put it in language students could understand.

One way to create a representative SLT at the middle or high school level is for the adult team to go into the cafeteria at lunchtime and invite one student from each table to become a member. More than likely, this taps a range of different types of students—in many schools, athletes will be at one table, Goth kids at another, Asian kids at one table, African American kids at another. At the elementary school level, teachers can consider the different groups in their school and invite members of each to create a truly representative student team.

Selecting "opinion leaders" from each table to be members of the leadership team is also a powerful strategy. If the students selected are prominent individuals among their peers, then they can easily talk about the issues, problems, or strengths of the students in their group. They can also easily disseminate the SLT's goals, work, and project ideas to their peer group. Once the student leadership team has come up with something to share with their peers, all the student leaders need do is sit down with their lunch mates and tell their friends about the leadership team's work.

Since student leaders are already "plugged in" to their particular peer group and already speak their language, these peers more readily understand and accept the work of the SLT. A diverse team has a much easier time gaining their peers' buy-in than they would if they were not already members of these diverse groups. When the student leadership team is truly representative of the entire population within the school, the team has greater access to and credibility with all students. Student engagement and cooperation with the team's projects and activities are thus more likely to occur.

Selecting only traditional student leaders—the popular, academically strong students—is unlikely to tap into the breadth of student experiences in the school. A straight-A student engaged in school will have insights into the teaching strategies that work well for her, but she may not understand the frustrations and obstacles to learning that other students might experience at the same school. If a student is a member of a racial majority group, he may have little real understanding of the kinds of challenges that a minority student might face in the same school or community.

The problem with picking only "successful" students for a leadership team is that it undermines the two most important leadership functions of the team: (1) obtaining wide ranging input from all students, and (2) achieving effective output or dissemination of student leadership ideas and initiatives throughout the school. *Student input* is the information, experiences, and wisdom that any student brings to a discussion about his or her own personal school experiences. At school, all students are a unique product of the day-to-day interactions they have with peers, teachers, school rules, procedures, the curriculum, and instructional practices. Obviously, no two students are alike. Members of certain social or academic groups, however, tend to have similar shared experiences. These groups may routinely see and or experience certain aspects of their school that members of other groups never experience.

If certain students have never had an encounter with the school's discipline system, then clearly they are unlikely to understand how effective (or ineffective) the school's policies may be in addressing students' behavioral problems. If students have never been targeted for social isolation or peer harassment, they may not know the shame, rage, or emotional pain these experiences produce, or how these incidents can dramatically interfere with learning and healthy development. We can only understand school climate through opportunities for student input on all of these issues. This expands our own individual (and limited) perspectives.

When collecting school climate data, it also helps to select student leaders who have personal connections with each of the main social and academic groups. Students are much more likely to take a survey seriously and provide valid information when asked by someone who looks and sounds like them. If the person asking for ideas has little in common with a student, the school climate survey is less likely to reflect accurate knowledge of experiences at the school.

When a school intentionally expands the membership of its SLT beyond only those students who are academically or socially successful, and includes students who are members of out-groups or targeted students who have firsthand experience with bullying, discrimination, school discipline, or academic struggles, it sends a clear message to students in the school that "this time something is different!" This also makes an important point to those students who are typically "on the outside looking in" that the adults in this school "get it." By reaching out to students who may fall outside of the territory of traditional leaders, the school's administration and teachers send a powerful message: They relay their desire to understand the school in new ways. They express genuine intentions to help each of their students succeed and have a voice in finding new ways to move the school forward. Developing a diverse SLT is a powerful way to accomplish the kind of shift in power relations that Sarason tells us is so important for successful school change.

PREVENTING PITFALLS: USE THE PURPLE BOX TO REPRESENT ALL SECTORS OF THE STUDENT BODY

The best way to ensure that your student leadership team is *ineffective* is to select the wrong students. Too many athletes, successful students, and "natural leaders" who do not have social links into diverse communities within the school (different racial, social, academic, or cultural groups) will make a team struggle. One group of students who are especially at risk of not being selected for a student leadership team are those who may be gay, lesbian, or transgendered. These students are often true experts on some troubling aspects of school climate because their peers so often socially isolate, bully, and harass them; many adults also often marginalize them.

A parent in Maine whose daughter was a closeted lesbian student suggested a great strategy for recruiting diverse teams of students. The student had tremendous fear of being "outed" and targeted for what was likely to be brutal peer harassment. No one in her school knew how difficult her life at school was, like the lives of so many other gay, lesbian, and transgendered kids. This parent had heard about the student leadership team and the school's commitment to improve school climate and respect. With these efforts, students like her daughter would be less adversely impacted by harassment, bullying, threats, and violence—they could get on with their life and learning.

This mom suggested that the only way her daughter would be able to become a member of the student leadership team would be if she could anonymously nominate herself. She asked us to develop a way for students who really wanted to be on the team to quietly let the adults know that they were interested. We came up with a purple box, placed outside of the guidance office with instructions on how anyone could nominate anyone else for consideration for team membership. Adults are always surprised at whose names end up in the purple box.

CHALLENGES TO CHOOSING A DIVERSE TEAM OF STUDENT LEADERS

Not everyone can immediately see the value of including this diverse group of students as school leaders or experts. The following story highlights a common knee-jerk response by teachers to the selection of diverse student leaders.

THESE KIDS AREN'T LEADERS: ONE TEACHER'S FRUSTRATIONS

Our students are so proud and excited to be part of this school improvement process. Their parents are proud of them too. In some cases, it's the first time these students have been told that their parents are proud of them. Being selected as members of this team has changed some of these students profoundly. They behave differently; they see themselves differently, and so do many of their peers. But there is still a problem with a few of our teachers.

When we announced the names of the students we had selected using MSA's diverse selection criteria, there were a number of teachers who spoke strongly against including some of these students. They said certain students were *not* leaders, that some didn't "deserve" to be on the team because of their poor grades or their past behavior. Now, these teachers say nasty things about the whole process because they do not see these kids as real "leaders."

In response, I keep focusing on how much these students offer us as experts on this school. When these teachers challenge us, I tell them how these students are sharing new ideas about the things we need to work on and do differently. I tell them how much we value their honesty and how the involvement of these students has helped their peers take this effort much more seriously. I keep trying to convince these teachers that just being on this team, in and of itself, is having an effect on these students' behavior, attitude, and confidence. I am afraid that these teachers are just stuck on the word *leaders* and these kids don't fit their mold. It's very frustrating.

Inviting disengaged or marginalized students to serve with more mainstream students on a student leadership team offers these students a fresh chance to become integrated into their school community. In some cases, it also offers an opportunity for these students to "fight back," in a constructive and productive way, against a system that has failed them and their peers. It empowers them to name the barriers that have impeded their success at school, and work to eliminate these obstacles to their learning and growth.

These nontraditional school leaders have told us that the invitation to join the student leadership team and participate in the real work of school reform has been an opportunity to restore their dignity and regain their faith in their school. In more than a few cases, teachers and guidance counselors who know these students well have told us, with tears in their eyes, that this opportunity has actually saved some of their students' lives. What can be more important than that?

MAKING IT REAL: STUDENT LEADERSHIP TRAINING

Student leaders we work with come from Grades 3–12. A productive size for most student leadership teams is between fifteen and twenty students. Since the numbers on a team may decline slightly when the work begins and attendance at meetings is required, it is good to start with a larger group. Typically, staff from MSA meet with the student team when it is first formed to begin team development and orient them to the reform work ahead. In this initial training,

- We explain the purpose of the team and expectations for team members as well as expectations for adults who will work with them.
- We lead activities that address topics such as the power of perception (since school climate is all about perception); the challenges of making, and sustaining, change in schools; the ecology of social groups in schools; what respectful teaching is; what engaged learning is; what empowerment means; how to work together with others who may be different; and how to make change happen.
- We ask students to tell their own personal stories about school climate and learning at their school. They begin by responding in writing to a set of open-ended prompts. These may include: "Describe the most respectful teacher in your school and what he or she does that feels respectful to you as a person and as a learner." "Describe what you feel are the 'unsafe places' at this school. What makes these places unsafe for you?" We then ask students to share their responses to these questions aloud with the rest of the team. This allows a better understanding of school climate issues and also helps the students begin to find their voices.
- To help them define school climate, we share the National School Climate Standards with students in language they can understand. We then ask the

students to share what they believe the purpose of their student leadership team ought to be. From this, we develop a few basic ground rules and a mission statement for the group's work.

- Some groups may want to brainstorm names for their leadership team to build group identity and to help others better understand who their team is and what they are trying to accomplish. It can take several meetings and more experience to agree on a good name. Some examples include Power Surge, The Dominoes, Chain Reaction, and Teachers and Students Working for Change (TASC).

- Finally, we show the student team how to log onto our SafeMeasures school climate surveys. We ask them to take the school climate survey before the rest of their peers do. We then teach them how to administer the survey to the rest of the students and teachers at their school. Providing the student leadership team with a powerful role and leadership task as one of the first things they do is a great way to kick-start the leadership team. The excitement of these third- through twelfth-grade students to do this important work is readily apparent; they can't wait to see what everybody says about their school experiences on the surveys.

CONCLUSION

Inviting a group of engaged and committed teachers to work with the administration as school climate leaders and designers is an empowering opportunity for teachers. The National School Climate Standards can provide a roadmap for these adult leaders to guide their journey toward developing a better school.

Picking a student to be a leader can change a life. Being chosen by adults to serve as a school leader and reformer can inspire any student to become more serious about his or her school experiences. Deep down, most of us want to believe that we can make a difference. Being chosen as a member of a student leadership team is an opportunity to make a real difference.

Students are truly the experts on the climate of respect and disrespect within their school. Diverse student leaders help adults and their peers understand their schools more deeply. Without these students' diverse perspectives, adults will not fully understand school climate and learning issues. By working with diverse student leaders, adults send every student a message that this time things are going to be different: "This time, your voice is going to be heard."

Choosing diverse students and teachers to serve as leaders also challenges many teachers' notions about what a leader is and who is capable of leadership. All of this can have a dramatic and almost immediate effect on school climate.

SIMPLE SUMMARY: STAGE ONE

- Enlist administrative support for shared leadership involving teachers and students.
- Create an adult design team and student leadership team with diverse representation.
- Facilitate leadership team training to develop group identity, clarify purposes and roles, and understand the collaborative action research process.
- Provide training for students to organize and supervise the schoolwide climate survey.

BOOK STUDY QUESTIONS

1. Who are the students picked for leadership positions at your school? Are these same kids picked often for other positive recognition at school? Which kids are never picked for leadership roles? Why not?

2. Consider the diversity of students at your school. Go to the cafeteria and see who sits with whom—what different groups exist? How do their school experiences differ?

3. How would school programs or practices need to change to respond to this varied range of perspectives, and ensure the success of every student? What programs or practices currently in place most benefit which students? Which students seem least well addressed by existing practices? What other practices might be applied that would work for these less well-served kids?

4

Stage Two: Including All Voices

School Climate Data Collection

Inquiry is fatal to certainty.

Will and Ariel Durant, *The Story of Civilization:
The Age of Faith* (1935, p. 1045)

THE IMPORTANCE OF DATA

Once a diverse team of student experts is carefully and strategically selected to serve as the adult design team's partner in working to improve school climate, the real work begins. The first task is collecting valid and reliable qualitative and quantitative school climate data. These data allow all students and their teachers the opportunity to communicate their perceptions and experiences related to the school's climate. When done correctly, schoolwide school climate data collection can send a clear message about the school's readiness to listen to what everyone has to say as they work to improve the school.

Collecting data on school climate is important in two ways. First, conducting a schoolwide inquiry to understand school climate is an exciting first leadership project to undertake for both the student and adult leadership teams. It is meaningful, challenging work that requires contributions from everybody. Data collection kick-starts the entire school climate leadership process. Secondly, school climate data that assess student and adult perceptions of school climate can reveal similarities and differences in perception about the school for all to see, discuss, and explore.

These data allow schools to address the following questions: How do adult and student perceptions about bullying and harassment compare? What is the range of viewpoints about a school's physical or emotional safety? How effective do those surveyed feel the school's discipline system may be? How much choice does the school provide to its students? How responsive is teaching to individual students? A comprehensive set of climate data, especially when data collection tools are aligned with accepted school climate standards, can reveal essential information to help begin the process of improving the school.

PREVENTING PITFALLS: AVOID HOMEMADE SURVEYS

There are many different "school climate-type" surveys available today. However, survey development is a rather tricky and technical business. The validity and reliability of homemade survey items is likely to be problematic. We have spent more than ten years designing our SafeMeasures school climate surveys for elementary, middle, high school students, teachers, and parents. (The Sample School Climate Data Summary in Appendix B illustrates the types of questions we have developed to assess essential school climate factors.) School leaders who wish to conduct school climate surveys should contact their state's department of education for a list of approved service providers they would recommend, along with possible funding sources that may be available to schools to support this work.

WHAT GETS MEASURED IS WHAT GETS DONE

The premise that decisions about the effectiveness of our schools ought to be based on valid information is an idea that is here to stay. No Child Left Behind set the stage for an unprecedented amount of academic data being collected in our nation's schools. We now spend weeks of each school year assessing students' academic knowledge and skills using standardized tests. Yet, as a nation, we haven't really wrestled with the question, "What should we be measuring and how should we be using data to make decisions that will improve our schools?" We need to ask ourselves if there are other important types of data that schools should be collecting and using to make decisions.

If what gets measured is what counts in schools, then it seems that one powerful strategy for changing schools would be to collect other kinds of important information along with academic test scores. If we believe that there needs to be a better balance between the academic development of our children and their personal, social, and emotional growth, then we must consider assessing students in each of these areas to determine their needs and document their progress.

This is precisely what the U.S. Department of Education (USDOE) is currently proposing, because school safety and climate are so central to student learning. As Kevin Jennings, the assistant deputy secretary of education for the Office of Safe and Drug-Free Schools, said at a recent conference we held in New Hampshire on school climate and learning,

> The Office of Safe and Drug-Free Schools is the smallest yet mightiest department in the USDOE, and as I tell the Secretary of Education and the other department heads, it is also the most important office in the DOE, because if students do not feel safe in school, then none of the other programs that relate to all other areas of education will work. (Jennings, 2010)

The Office of Safe and Drug-Free Schools is asking all schools to begin to evaluate school climate, safety, and student engagement as part of their annual testing procedures. The belief is that if schools are required to report on bullying and harassment, the prevalence of positive relationships among students and teachers, and the climate of respect, then schools will begin to take more effective action related to these fundamental issues.

Adding valid and reliable school climate data to the assessment mix offers a whole new set of valuable data to consider for shaping a school's polices, programs, and practices. When adults and students begin collecting and looking carefully at school climate data, they quickly see that there is much to think about and much work to do to make their schools safe, respectful, rigorous, and relevant learning centers for all children.

SOME POTENTIAL PROBLEMS WITH SCHOOL DATA COLLECTION

For nearly fifteen years, I, Bill, taught seventh-grade social studies and watched thousands of students take standardized tests and surveys in school. When starting a survey, one of the first questions my students asked was, "Will this count on our grade?" When they learned that the answer was no, many students simply did not take these tests or surveys seriously. We have all heard stories of schools that have begun to offer students treats and incentives for working their hardest or performing well on state tests. Are there less coercive ways to get students to want to complete surveys candidly so that their voices can be heard?

As more schools are beginning to assess school climate or other social and emotional issues, these surveys, on top of all the other academic testing, cause many "overtested" students to simply write off these inquiries as irrelevant. Too often, some students may not even read the questions before checking off their answers.

Some surveys are simply too daunting for children. We recently reviewed one lengthy bullying and student perceptions survey designed for elementary school students that contained more than eighty multiple-choice items. The reading level was far above the norm for the average fifth grader, yet was being administered to students as young as third grade. How useful would the information gathered from such a test really be to a school?

We often work with educators who tell us they don't need to do school climate surveys because they have already collected this kind of data from their students. In one recent case, we asked to see the results of one such survey, and the data were over three years old. We asked the principals and teachers if they had ever looked at the results of the student and teacher surveys or used the information in any way. None of them had looked at the results. Unfortunately, all too often, a school collects data but no one bothers to use them.

We believe the reason that school leaders continue to collect data, even if they never analyze or use the results, is that collecting data, in and of itself, is sometimes viewed as an important leadership strategy. Collecting data shows an interest in making "data-driven" decisions and (perhaps) doing something about issues raised by the data. To not go back and use that information, due to lack of time or simply lack of follow-through, is a powerful statement about what really matters to these school leaders.

WHAT AND HOW TO MEASURE

If schools are now expected to assess school climate, two questions naturally arise: (1) What will a school choose to measure? (2) How will the school assure reliable collection of data?

The methods used most commonly to collect school climate data—and other important information—raise concerns. We know that when adults such as teachers, the school resource officer, or the principal administer student surveys, students react powerfully to the person at the front of the room. Many students have told us that they alter their answers to survey questions according to what they think the person asking the questions seeks. So, the methodology used to collect school climate data from students, teachers, and parents matters a great deal.

Research on SAT administrator effects on student performance provides a useful lesson on the importance of survey administration methodology.

In essence, the students taking the SAT who physically resembled (by race and gender) the person administering the test did significantly better on the SAT than did those who did not look like the test administrator (Dambrun & Taylor, 2005). This is instructive for school climate survey administration. We believe that school climate surveys produce the most valid results when a representative team of student leaders from diverse academic, racial, and economic backgrounds administer them.

WHAT TO DO WITH DATA

Sometimes, even if a school collects climate data, the most important question is "What happens next?" One state recently made it a statewide educational priority to collect data on student perceptions of their school experiences. Initially, we applauded that decision. Schools in this state were prodded by their department of education (DOE) and offered significant resources to collect important school climate data from students and teachers. Following administration of these surveys, a summary of results was provided to schools, and school leaders did as they were required by the state—reporting their school's results to the school board, parents, and the local community.

Anyone who has ever surveyed students and teachers can attest that there are going to be significant perceptual differences between the students and the adults. (Any parent of a teenager also knows this.) So, it was not surprising that many principals, teachers, and school boards soon began to complain because the results were often negative. These leaders saw the surveys as just providing critics such as students, parents, and the community with another opportunity to find fault with schools.

Without the state DOE providing schools a clear process for addressing the student perceptual data they gathered, it was inevitable that the results would simply be seen as students "complaining." Indeed, several school leaders told me, Bill, that they were never going to survey students again, because all this did was cause problems with the community.

I expressed my concerns to the deputy commissioner of education because I felt that this process (or lack thereof) was giving a bad rap to the whole idea of student voice in schools. Administrators were actually planning to reduce student input in the future as a result of the flack this poorly designed process generated. After a few years of giving the public "bad news" about their public schools, the state eventually stopped funding this kind of data collection and moved its focus elsewhere.

The truth is that these student data could have been an excellent way to address long-standing problems in these schools. What was missing, however, was follow-through after the data were collected. The data were used, as the principals said, in a "summative" fashion; they were used primarily to label a school as being successful or unsuccessful; parents, students, and communities then judged the performance of the schools based on these conclusions.

We believe it is essential from the start to make clear that any data representing different perceptions of the school need to be carefully examined, discussed, interpreted, and acted upon with caution. School climate data should not be used simply to pass judgment on the quality of a school, but rather to precipitate dialogue about the meaning of results, and to begin framing a prudent and responsible response to those issues the data reveal.

WHEN STUDENTS BECOME SCHOOL CLIMATE RESEARCHERS

As discussed previously, engaging in a process to better understand school climate issues presents powerful leadership opportunities for students and adults. When we invite students to collect and analyze their school's data, especially those who may have never been selected to take leadership roles before, they generally jump at the honor. Students tell us that being a researcher is a "pretty cool gig." The role of researcher is highly respected in our society. When we think of a researcher, we imagine a scientist at a microscope, a doctor giving experimental medicines trying to save a life, or a graduate student working over piles of data late into the night. When asked if they want to learn to be researchers, invariably students say, "yes!"

When student leaders figure out that it is mostly college students, graduate students, and adults who do research, they immediately take pride in taking on this mature role. Creating powerful roles for students is one of the most potent strategies for changing school climate and transforming students' self-perceptions. This works for student leadership teams, but it also works for students in the classroom (watch any elementary school class when asked, "Who wants to be line leader?").

Over the past twenty years, we have repeatedly witnessed the transformative power of providing young people with new and different roles. Research on role theory shows how being placed into new roles can dramatically affect a person's self-perception and alter behavior (Haney, Banks, & Zimbardo, 1973; Sherif & Sherif, 1956). One of the most famous studies, the Stanford Prison Experiment (as cited in Haney, Banks, & Zimbardo, 1973), showed how even randomly selected college students could quickly become aggressive and controlling when put in the role of prison guards. In less than two days, this experiment set up in the basement of the psychology lab had to be cancelled because the students playing the roles of prisoners suffered powerful psychological and emotional duress.

A more mainstream example of the way roles change how people act occurs with putting on a costume or mask. Observations at Mardi Gras, or even a Halloween party, reveal people who act in ways that defy the personality they emanate in "the real world." Jane Elliot's (1968) classic blue eyes/brown eyes exercise has also shown the power of roles and role reversals to help children and adults develop greater understanding and deepen their empathy toward others.

Giving students the role of researcher in the collaborative action research process not only changes the student's self-image, but it also facilitates more reliable data collection from their peers, who, for a change, see themselves as part of the assessment process.

THE POWER OF QUALITATIVE DATA

When students join the student leadership team, we explain that they are the real experts on the social, emotional, and academic climate inside their schools. (The role of expert on what school is like for them is one role that they take to immediately.) We ask them each to do some writing when they first come to the initial student leader's training. They answer questions about their own experiences with respect and disrespect at school, bullying they've witnessed or experienced personally, and engaging or not so engaging teaching methods. We then hold a focus group (a fancy research term for a discussion).

The students take turns telling each other and our staff wonderful and horrific stories about their school experiences. We try to capture their exact words in our notes from these focus groups, using this as our initial set of school climate data. These important stories are later carefully analyzed and shared with adults and peers as the SafeMeasures™ process unfolds.

Qualitative school climate data can reveal the most personal, emotional, and sometimes frightening realities of what happens to individual children inside a school every day. It is no wonder that some students struggle to learn when they are forced to endure what these stories and words reveal.

Student qualitative data can illustrate both simple and complex problems within schools. For example, sharing a student insight can raise relatively uncomplicated problems and their solutions (Preble & Knowles, 2011):

> One thing I would change about my school would be the amount of time we have to switch classes. We only have two minutes to go to the bathroom, grab everything you need for the next class, and talk with friends. If we got five minutes to do all this, I think we could get better grades because we wouldn't end up leaving our homework in our lockers.

But some quotes reveal much deeper challenges and choices facing teachers, students, and schools:

> Our school is a place where I am forced to come, without any choice on my part. I am told mostly what classes I will take. . . . Much of the material being learned I feel is arbitrary and busy-work, and won't help us to do what we really want to do [in our lives]. . . . So much time is spent doing things students hate to do and don't learn from.

Responses like this help teachers reflect on their work as educators, resulting in important dialogue about the work students are asked to complete, and the purpose behind much of what passes for "schooling." Qualitative data can reveal qualities of school climate, respect, and learning that no number or statistic can communicate as effectively. We try, then, to show teachers and students that they should never underestimate the power of words—whether kind or cruel.

SAMPLE QUALITATIVE DATA

"Every day I have to find a different route to class because the same group of kids are always waiting to harass me. They call me 'fag' and 'gay' and shove me into walls. The other day, I got to my car and they had smashed my windshield and left a sign saying, 'This is a fag's car.'"

"I think you need to know that a lot of the students have tried to hit or kick me in the past and it needs to stop."

"In front of teachers, students act respectful, but the majority of students are disrespectful and rude behind the teachers' backs."

"Teachers are respectful to some, but there are some students that the teachers don't even see. These students don't get any attention."

"If kids see bullying, they walk away because it just brings up trouble to get involved."

"Kids who get bullied need to fight their own battles."

"If you ignore the cool kids, it's ok. If you stand up to them, you get pushed around."

The power of these quotes is compelling. We believe that data like these serve as an essential tool for teachers, student leaders, and administrators. In looking at the effects of school climate on students and their learning, they discover that they each have a personal and emotional stake. These data help school leaders and teachers look at school climate as something that actually plays itself out one student at a time, one incident at a time, every day, every week, and every year that a student is in that school.

When a single student gets bullied to the point where she takes her own life, then everybody suddenly sees that this work is essential. The words and stories of individual students should be a powerful wake-up call for adults and students alike—they show us that this matters.

Using individual quotes from focus groups or surveys is also a powerful strategy to make emotional connections with teachers or students. Qualitative data are great for touching the hearts, minds, and imaginations of teachers, students, and administrators. Powerful words taken from the qualitative data can serve as a potent tool for lending urgency. They also help build teacher engagement and commitment to the work of school climate improvement.

THE VALUE OF QUANTITATIVE DATA

Of the more than 50,000 students we have surveyed over the past ten years, fewer than 30 percent "agree" or "strongly agree" that they "have opportunities to make choices" about the things they do or study in their classes. In these same schools, typically over 90 percent of teachers report that they give students choices in class. Clearly, numbers and statistics across an entire population of students or teachers hold a very different kind of power than do the words of an individual.

In order to gain a broader and more generalized understanding of school climate, we use quantitative research methods that include schoolwide student and teacher surveys. Where schools want to look further and deeper, we survey parents as well. We have developed a set of student, teacher, and parent school climate surveys and self-assessment tools for this purpose based on our beeper study research, hundreds of student interviews, focus groups, and the National School Climate Standards (NSCC, 2009) discussed in the previous chapter.

After the training with the college researchers, student leaders are ready to administer the online surveys to every student and teacher in their school, inviting each to express what they know about school climate and respect in the school.

To administer the surveys, we group student leaders in diverse pairs. This mixed pairing models the cooperative relationships between different groups of students that the team is trying to achieve within the whole school. The adventure of conducting school climate research on an entire school is a wonderful team-building activity for a diverse student leadership team. In addition, it is fun for the students, and a relatively easy project to schedule and implement.

The student leaders can expertly set up access to computers in the library or computer labs. They learn to bring up the online surveys in no time. They welcome their fellow students into the room and, as modeled for them when they took the surveys themselves, carefully read them the standardized instructions. The leaders inform their peers of the student leadership team's name, mission, and the purpose of the survey. They explain that it will be their job as leadership team members to bring the final results of the survey back to their peers and the adults in their school, and to ensure that student voices are heard as part of this school improvement process.

Most students are impressed to learn from the SLT that their input and voices are important. Students appreciate being given a choice about completing the surveys. In almost every case, students willingly and respectfully answer the survey. We believe this is another testament to a shift in power relations from typical adult-administered surveys to student-led action research.

The student leaders also invite the teachers, who come to the lab with their class, to take their own version of the survey (in part to ensure that teachers are not walking around looking at students' responses). Almost no one "goofs off" on the survey using this approach; they generally answer questions seriously. We believe that this process not only provides a powerful initial leadership role for the SLT, but it also yields more valid and reliable data from students and teachers to be used for comparative analysis of school climate issues.

The survey results provide student leaders and their adult collaborators with an empirical version of student voice. We have found that adults are more likely to reflect forthrightly about their school when students' perceptions of their own school are communicated effectively using valid and reliable school climate survey data. Students' stories, along with generalizable, valid, and reliable quantitative data, provide a powerful, mixed-method assessment of school climate. The job of collecting these data across an entire school is a rigorous and empowering experience for student leaders. It brings them closer together as a team and prepares them for the work ahead. It is predictably common that immediately after surveys are completed for an entire school, at least one student leader will ask, "So when do we get to see what everybody said?" What schools do with these data is the next and most important step—making sense of the results and using them to take action to improve a school.

MAKING IT REAL: ELEMENTARY SCHOOL STUDENT RESEARCHERS

Ellen Ahyon, a behavioral specialist at Coral Spring Elementary School (CSES), in Florida, is as energetic as you get. She is passionate about her school and a tireless advocate for her students. To address problems they were having with bullying and school climate in general, Ellen asked her principal, Renee Shaw, if she would be willing to try the SafeMeasures process at their school for students with severe emotional and behavioral problems. After learning about the process, Renee enthusiastically agreed.

Ellen asked teachers to nominate a representative group of students in Grades 3–5 for the soon to be formed student leadership team. Immediately, the teachers asked whether they could include names of students with behavioral problems. When Ellen said emphatically, "Yes!" a number of teachers balked. How could a leadership team even *be* a leadership team with "these kind of students" on it? The words *leader* and *behavior problems* didn't seem to fit together at all.

After Ellen's energetic lobbying, eighteen students were assembled. The team was young and excited, with a good representation from Grades 3–5. The team was racially and ethnically diverse, reflecting their school and their Florida community. At their first meeting, the kids were curious about why they were there. They had many great questions about what they would be doing. During the initial leadership training games, there was not a single problem with student behavior. Afterwards, I, Bill, asked Ellen if she had decided not to include the students with behavior problems. "Are you kidding me?" she laughed, "Lots of these are *my* kids!" And she beamed with that knowing told-you-so look.

The next morning, we brought the group back together, asked them to do some writing about school issues, and then we administered the school climate survey to the team. Ellen's colleagues, two teachers who had volunteered to mentor the team with Ellen, had to help a few students with some of the words and in one case, a teacher translated the English questions into Spanish for a student. But it all worked well.

After a break for lunch, we set up three mobile computer labs. Student leaders, who were trained that morning to administer the surveys, came back in their teams of four for their shift administering the surveys to three classes. These leaders became very serious as they awaited their peers who were on their way down to complete the surveys.

The mixed groups of third, fourth, and fifth graders welcomed their peers to the makeshift computer labs. They introduced themselves as members of the student leadership team (quite proudly, I must say) and reviewed the instructions for completing the surveys step by step. They seemed to relish the part where they told the students that they didn't *have* to take the survey; it was completely voluntary and no one would see their answers, so whatever they had to say about their school would be a secret (they liked the word *secret* better than anonymous). Every student began completing the survey.

After a short time, I noticed that on one student's computer screen the answers to the first few questions were already filled in. "Everybody stop!" I said. Ellen and I spoke rather frantically about what was going on here. Why would there be answers already completed on a few computer screens? Within a few seconds, Samier, a fourth grader, said, "I know, it's in the cache." I had no idea what he was talking about.

This was at a time when we had just gone from paper-and-pencil surveys to online surveys and I was a mess. "Here . . . you just need to do this," the little boy said. Whatever the heck he did, it worked! He pressed a few buttons, rebooted, and we were off and running. All this took less than five minutes and we had no more problems for the rest of the day. Samier had saved the day—I owed my professional credibility to a fourth grader.

Never underestimate what a child is capable of doing. That was clearly the lesson I learned that day at CSES. All these PhDs were standing around scratching their heads, and Samier took charge and solved the problem. What was wonderful about what happened at CSES was that those teachers who had resisted inviting "behavior" students to be on the leadership team learned this lesson too.

After we collected survey data from all the students and their teachers, our research assistants collated the data and sent the results in graph form back down to Renee, Ellen, and the CSES team. I later flew back and met with the student leadership team again to go over their results, set goals for improving school climate at CSES, and develop action plans to address the issues that we found. Ellen had taken the graphic data summaries we typically provide and blew them up into large posters. The students used colored markers to make notes and circle the numbers that they thought were more important. (Pictures of the CSES team doing this work can be seen on our website at www.thecscl.org.) I remember one of Ellen's students saying, "Hey, this is what we did for the FCAT Test!" as he was reading the bar graphs and choosing the evidence that illustrated his school's strengths and its biggest problems.

After school that day, the student leadership team stayed to meet with the faculty to help lead the adults through the exact same process they had just completed. They introduced themselves again, very proudly, and told the teachers that they had some work that the teachers needed to do. "Don't worry," one little girl said, "we already did it and we will help you." And that is just what happened. The students presented their big charts, showing the key findings that they had identified in their data, and they instructed the teachers that they needed to do the same thing.

During that meeting, Ellen and her colleagues told stories to the teachers about the work of the student leadership team. I told them how Samier had saved my reputation. One of the mentors, who had worked with the students collecting data, told how a little third grader named Malika stepped up to help her peers. When administering the survey, Malika had noticed a few students were having trouble reading the items. Recalling how the adult mentors had sat next to the student leaders who needed help and read the questions softly aloud to them, Malika knelt down between these two boys, read the items aloud to one boy on her right and translated the questions into Spanish for the other student on her left—*at the same time.* Malika and Samier were both among Ellen's "behaviorally challenged" kids.

The students helped the teachers come up with a shared set of school climate improvement goals, agreeing on what they together needed to work on to improve their school.

Needless to say, the student leaders were a big hit that day at that faculty meeting. Afterwards, several teachers approached Ellen and apologized for doubting that her students could serve in these leadership roles. Sheepishly, they admitted they had underestimated these students' abilities.

Source: Dr. Ellen Ahyon, Behavioral Specialist, Coral Spring Elementary School, Coral Spring, FL.

CONCLUSION

While the act of gathering qualitative and quantitative school climate data is empowering, the data themselves are essential to give school leaders, parents, students, and teachers a vivid picture of their school. When school climate data—in the form of individual students' stories, teacher and student survey data, disciplinary incident reports, student attendance data, and academic test results—are assembled, the data can paint a comprehensive picture of a school's greatest strengths and needs. The next step is to collectively determine what all this information means.

SIMPLE SUMMARY: STAGE TWO

- Explain the process and goals of the project to student leaders.
- Explain and emphasize the importance of the student roles in this process—they can help their peers share what school is really like for all students at the school; they can get their peers to take this survey seriously; they can bring ideas to adults that will really help to change how their school does things.
- Prepare student leaders to lead survey administration.
- Collect survey data from all students and teachers.
- Collect focus group data from student leadership team (if it is truly a diverse team).

BOOK STUDY QUESTIONS

1. What insights could you get from students' perspectives on learning and what could be improved that you can't get just by talking to teachers?

2. How much time is spent in your school on standardized testing? How much time is spent asking students and teachers what can help them be more effective teachers and learners? Would time invested in the latter perhaps improve results in the former?

3. Try asking students to write freely on these experiences in school. Ask one or more of your students to ask their peers the same questions with the stipulation that these students will collect the answers and analyze them. See if the results differ. What insights do you get from the student responses in both cases?

4. In your school, how often do adults consider the different perspectives held by different individual kids? How often do you generalize about how kids are doing or what the students think? How would looking from the lens of individual students' perspectives change your understanding of students' experiences with school?

5. How do different individual students experience school? How can you constructively respond to the one or two students whose experiences may be much less positive than for others?

Stage Three: Thinking Together

Data Analysis and Goal Setting

Making decisions based on data is very common for all of us—weather reports, grocery prices, stock markets, and doctor's visits all involve data. Yet, in education, we often make many decisions based entirely on supposition and intuition.

Florida Center for Instructional Technology,
Using Data to Make Decisions (n.d.)

NEW SHOES, LESS GOSSIP

Like so many schools, Lisbon Elementary School's survey data showed that both teachers and students thought there was a bullying problem. The teachers and the student leaders wanted to address their perceived problem with bullying, but the question was, where to begin?

Working with SafeMeasures brought a diverse team of student leaders into the conversation, by which this team of charmingly cute third, fourth, and fifth graders was invited to share their understanding of the issue of bullying in their school with their teachers.

The students pointed out that there were really only a handful of bullies, whom they could easily name in quick order. The students also observed that in many cases, these same students were also the targets of bullying.

Ms. James, the well-liked third-grade teacher, asked the students, "Where does the bullying happen?" The students quickly agreed, "On the playground." Teachers and students debated this point for some time, because it seemed that the majority of teachers assumed all along that the vast majority of bullying behavior was happening on the bus.

"And what do you think we should do to stop the bullying on the playground?" another teacher asked.

Benny, a fidgety, mop-headed ten-year-old, blurted out, "Get the teachers new shoes!" All the students laughed and nodded vigorously, knowing those fancy high heels would never venture far from the protected confines of the covered walkway.

"Stop the playground teachers from gossiping together!" another student said, and again, laughter erupted from the teachers and students.

"Make the teachers stand at least twenty-five feet apart and make them stand here, and here, and here," said one student who had drawn a map of the playground. He pointed to the spots where he knew the teachers should be positioned if they wanted to see what was really happening on the playground.

"What's this?" asked a teacher who was pointing to some marks on the student's map of the playground.

"That's the big snow pile," said the mapmaker. "All the bullies do it behind the snow pile, and the recess teachers never go back there."

A knowing, guilty look came over the faces of the teachers, accompanied by nervous laughter. The clues to the bullying mystery at this school were becoming very clear in a matter of minutes: new shoes, twenty-five feet between teachers, no distracting chatting, and attention to what was going on behind the snow pile.

Then came the final clue. "When is this happening, morning bus recess or lunch recess?" asked a teacher who looked like she already knew the answer.

"Lunch recess!" every student exclaimed in perfect unison, beaming that they knew the answers to these easy questions, knowing full well that they were indeed *experts* on this subject.

After the students had left, the teachers were abuzz with discussion about what they had learned from these elementary school students. It quickly became clear that the teachers could readily address the bullying problem that they now knew was happening on the lunch playground. They could now see the real problem and its surprisingly limited scope.

The decision about how to prevent bullying thus fell squarely on the teachers and principal's shoulders, because as it turns out, there were no teachers on the playground during lunch recess anymore. Teachers had gotten the principal to excuse them from lunch recess duties, to allow time for common planning. It appears that no one had trained the teacher's aides who were now supervising students on the playground. In the end, with help from their students and their data, many teachers concluded that the problem wasn't really bullying at all, it was a problem of adult supervision. The teachers as a whole then had to decide, was their goal for improving school climate going to be stopping students from bullying, or was it going to be that adults would work together to improve playground supervision?

INTERNAL OR EXTERNAL LOCUS OF CONTROL: WHOSE RESPONSIBILITY?

Before meeting with the student leadership team at Lisbon, several veteran teachers had already framed a solution to what they saw as their bullying problem. These teachers proposed to the principal that he should approve a series of weekly all-school assemblies on bullying. They had decided that all elementary students should come down to the cafeteria, every Friday afternoon, for an anti-bullying assembly that would consist of readings, presentations, videos, and activities to raise awareness among all students about the dangers and damages caused by students who bully. This was not necessarily a bad idea, but the point we wish to make here is how easily some teachers can jump to a solution before seeking to understand the nature of the problem itself.

Some teachers still felt this assembly idea was exactly what was needed to stop bullying, even after the students showed them that the primary concern was just with a handful of poorly supervised students, during one small part of the school day. What is it about teachers who are so determined to "solve" a problem, using traditional approaches like assemblies to try to "fix the kids," without really seeking to better understand the root of the problem?

This is the point where *teacher culture* within a school enters the picture. Teachers' collective beliefs, sense of personal and professional efficacy, and mental models of deeply engrained assumptions about schooling, teaching, and learning greatly affect how they approach all aspects of their work (Caine & Caine, 1997).

A handful of these teachers were unable to shift their perspective from teaching all students not to be bullies, as the way to address this problem, to teaching adults to better supervise the playground. In the first instance, it is students and their bullying behavior that is held as the problem. In the second case, it is the teachers' responsibility for the problem that is at the heart of the issue at hand. This is classic internalized or externalized *locus of control*. Is it someone else's fault that this problem exists (external), or is it something *I can change* (internal)?

We know that teachers with high levels of efficacy tend toward internalized locus of control. They see themselves as the answer to a student's individual needs and challenges. They believe in their own training, skills, time, and effort as the keys to their students' success, and their own accomplishments as educators. If they can understand the issues, they have the capacity to solve them. Accurately understanding the issues in one's school becomes key to improving climate and learning. We know that effective teacher collaboration to solve school problems and improve school climate can have a positive impact on the *collective efficacy* of a teaching staff (Moore & Esselman, 1992).

COGNITIVE DISSONANCE: WRESTLING WITH DATA TO CONSTRUCT MEANING

In Stage Three of the SafeMeasures™ process, school climate meets teacher culture head-on. This stage of data analysis and goal setting has everything to do with teachers learning about the school climate issues and needs that are most prevalent in their school. The first two stages of forming student and adult leadership teams and conducting schoolwide surveys are relatively easy and nonthreatening leadership tasks. While it may be a bit unfamiliar to include students in the process and to ask for feedback from all teachers and students, not much about school norms needs to change to take these first steps as a school begins its journey to improve school climate.

In Stage Three, schools look closely at their school climate data. This examination of a school's climate from student, teacher, and parent perspectives can be (and usually is) a bit of an awakening at most schools. With honest introspection, most people in any school would admit there are obviously areas for improvement. Confronting this reality in concrete terms—with words and numbers identifying specifically these shortcomings everyone knows exist—can lead some to defensiveness, criticism, and denial. For others, it provides the evidence they have been looking for to point out what, to them, are persistent flaws, problems, or issues. The evidence illustrates that it is finally time to address the issues head-on.

PREVENTING PITFALLS: AVOID DEFENSIVENESS AND DENIAL

Invariably, some of the data from climate surveys surprise certain adults. At the least, there will be some discrepancies between student and teacher responses. This can lead some teachers to question these results. Reminding everyone of the integrity of the data collection process before they see the data can help. More important, assuring a no-fault culture and emphasizing the task is not to "solve" the worst numbers, but to use the data to identify school goals helps deflect attention from denying any particular piece of data. Leadership teams need to choose the data they find most worth addressing and achievable at this point. This can mean not aiming for the most challenging issues first but prioritizing ones that the students and teachers find most pressing.

A key part of learning in any setting is some degree of cognitive dissonance—a discovery of something new that confronts a prior belief or understanding. For organizational change to happen, this cognitive dissonance is even more essential as a disruption occurs between the way things have always worked and what actually needs to happen to make positive change. As countless books on organizational change tell us, many people shy away from change, and even more avoid conflict. Facing dissonance almost intentionally would seem ill-advised, but it is exactly this kind of "creative tension," structured in a safe and thoughtful process, that forms the power to change the all-too-often accepted shortcomings of our schools.

Focus groups and open-ended survey questions provide students and adults with opportunities to speak their minds and tell their own truths about what is happening inside their school. While this information can be helpful, these individual, often personal, comments can result in some difficult and pointed criticisms being expressed. Using data productively to inspire introspection, learning, and change takes skill and tact.

NO FAULT, NO BLAME

We strive to make sure that teachers and administrators accept the feedback from their school's climate data as constructive feedback rather than judgmental criticism. It can sometimes be difficult for principals and teachers to hear certain kinds of feedback without responding emotionally, even if the substance behind the comments is worth considering. For this reason, it is important to start the process of reviewing and analyzing data with a "no fault, no blame" agreement (Cohen & Elias, 2010).

The purpose of the action research process is not to assign blame or find fault, but rather to use data *formatively* to initiate dialogue and action. This in turn addresses important issues, systemic problems, and organizational needs. We always try to emphasize that we are looking not at any individual piece of evidence. Rather, we look for patterns in the data; themes that reoccur are the indicators of a problem worthy of the group's time and attention. This can depersonalize the results, allowing teachers to be less defensive and more open to analyzing the data, sorting out conflicting perceptions, and honestly reflecting on the challenges in their school.

Key to this process is students' and teachers' shared involvement. By themselves, teachers might be able to explain away issues that the data raised. They may offer intellectual critiques of data collection methods or rationalized blame about the "educational system," or even prejudicial or discriminatory remarks about the inevitable weaknesses of certain children or families. When sitting together with students, who share the same desire as teachers to make the school an effective learning environment, teachers are led back to their best instincts—to the roots of the mission that originally called them to teaching—to serve the interests of children and society. With students sitting at the table, teachers almost invariably become better listeners and learners.

WORDS OR NUMBERS? ANALYZING DATA WITH STUDENTS

Social science research is generally divided into quantitative (numbers) and qualitative (words) methods. While numbers seem more objective and concrete, words can often prove to be more emotionally powerful and inspiring when it comes to getting the attention of both students and adults. In the SafeMeasures process, we employ both words and numbers to provide the most vivid, complete, and accurate picture of the things that go on every day inside a particular school. This picture can inspire or inhibit learning and growth.

In practice, we find that, in any leadership group of students, teachers, administrators, or parents, there are always some individuals who are "numbers people" and some who prefer words. In fact, when we ask who would like to look at the qualitative school climate data (individual student and teacher quotes and writing) and who wants to look at the numerical data (statistics, graphs, etc.), the breakdown is almost always about even, with equal numbers attracted to each form of data.

The first time we look at the data in the school, we work with the student leadership team separately from the teachers. The reason for this is to empower students to develop confidence and expertise that they can build on when they begin their subsequent work with their teachers. Given the power asymmetry between students and teachers in traditional schooling, if students are to work productively with adults, they need this "leg up" to feel grounded in their data analysis skills and the conclusions they draw. So, we begin Stage Three by sharing qualitative and quantitative school climate data with the student leadership team.

In working with the student team, we bring a data summary that has overall results for each question on the survey, along with subcategories to compare data for teachers and students, college bound and noncollege bound, boys and girls, by grade, as well as other demographic distinctions asked for by the school. We also bring a summary of student responses to open-ended questions on the survey, providing hundreds of individual statements written in response to the final question on the survey, "Is there anything else you would like to share with us about your school and how well it is working for you?"

After dividing up the team by word or number preference, we ask the numbers group to go through the statistical data and look for anything that jumps out at them as showing a great success or a potential problem in their school. Students assiduously take out highlighters and mark up their data summaries, working with a seriousness usually reserved for only the most consequential exams.

Discussing one standard at a time, the adult facilitator then asks the students what they highlighted. "The numbers on Question 44, 'Girls are treated with respect by other girls' are really low," says a heavily pierced girl with jet-black hair and all black clothes. An athletic looking boy adds, "I circled the question, 'I often hear students make hurtful comments about other students.' Only 12 percent of our teachers say that they hear kids making these hurtful comments to each other, but 63 percent of kids say they hear these things a lot." With prompting, a shy-looking boy in shabby clothes asks, "I picked this one—'kids treat teachers with respect'—77 percent of teachers agree kids are respectful to them but just 32 percent of students agree. What's with that?"

We advise to not necessarily look for the "worst" numbers or the "biggest problems," but rather look for issues the data indicate are worth addressing. Usually, within each standard, the data cluster around a more general theme—for example, under Standard 3 on effective teaching and learning, the students might point out low numbers of students who feel there are enough *choices* within classes, that *teachers really know student's interests,* and that a variety of *different teaching methods* are used in their classes. The SLT might describe these factors together as "need better teaching."

Lack of respect for teachers, students not being invited to offer suggestions about things that need to improve at school, and teachers not taking time to learn about individual students' interests and goals might be labeled "lack of respect for others." These clusters of issues, once named, can then be expressed as goals with more positive, forward-looking terminology.

The qualitative data, or words group, has a similar task but with more nuanced data. We ask this group to highlight the most powerful quotes they feel the teachers need to hear to really understand what students are exposed to every day in the school. The words group is equally serious about this task, finding statements that resonate with them personally. They each select three or four of their top student quotes that will be read aloud in front of their teachers at the beginning of the data analysis faculty meeting later that day. They often choose quotes that "speak truth to power" ("This school is like a prison," "We never get to choose the things we learn about."). Or, they choose positive examples of what their favorite teachers do that students really appreciate ("Miss B. always lets us choose the books we read and write about in class," "Mr. J. uses a SMART Board to teach us math and it makes learning much more fun for me. I also learn it way better that way."). The collection of quotes from their peers helps the student team express, from a student perspective, the diverse experiences of individuals in the school.

Quantitative data can mask individual viewpoints in overall statistics— maybe 95 percent of the students feel totally safe at school, but one or two, maybe those with unique characteristics (e.g., the only two Muslim kids, or out lesbians, or non-native English speakers) feel threatened continually.

The qualitative data, which provide more individual perspectives, can bear witness to these personal viewpoints, and amplify voices that may be totally silenced in the general life of the school.

We ask words-group participants to each choose several quotes they find most powerful, and then students aggregate these into themes. To check the validity of the data, we compare themes from the words and numbers groups. Although there are sometimes subtle differences in phrasing, in most cases, the themes evident in the numbers are supported and elucidated by the words. Together, the numerical statistics combined with the students' evocative offer a convincing, data-based case for the issues the students feel a need to address.

PREVENTING PITFALLS: AVOID LOOKING AT ITEMS IN ISOLATION

Good research is based on *triangulation*—looking for patterns from different data and different methods of data collection. The qualitative data should confirm (or disconfirm) trends identified in the quantitative data. Although a student group might look at the quotes separate from the numbers group, be sure to bring both groups together to see how the numbers and quotes match up. If they don't reinforce each other, that too is an intriguing exercise to try to understand why they differ.

USING QUANTITATIVE DATA EFFECTIVELY

In the world of school accountability, for most people, objective measures and numbers are what really count. It makes sense, then, that we would gather quantifiable, numeric data to assess and draw conclusions about how respectful or disrespectful a school feels for its students, teachers, parents, and community. Valid and reliable surveys add an important dimension to the school climate picture. Many schools and districts are beginning to collect and use school climate data in tandem with student academic data to gain a more holistic and deeper understanding of how their school is working. This climate data offer context for all other data analysis about school functioning. Without data on school climate, choosing interventions for bullying prevention, improved discipline, or even better academic performance is mostly shooting in the dark.

With climate data collected from student and teacher surveys, we report the results back to schools using comprehensive, comparative data summaries. These data summaries allow a school to compare responses of different groups, such as student and teacher, on each question. (See Appendix B: Sample School Climate Data Summary.)

Our school climate surveys ask each child to indicate his or her post–high school educational plans. While we don't assume these student aspirations will be 100 percent accurate, they tell us something potentially important about each child's life in school. In the school climate data we have collected, there are often significant differences between school experiences of college-bound and noncollege-bound students. One factor behind these differences may be a student's socioeconomic status. Data showing these differences prompt provocative discussions among adults and students about the possible reasons behind such differences.

PREVENTING PITFALLS: HONESTLY ASSESS LIMITATIONS

Some data will just jump out at you and make you see things differently in an instant. Within thirty seconds of looking at her middle school's quantitative data summary, one teacher exclaimed out loud "Look how many of these kids want to go to college!" She admitted her amazement that she never talked about college to her students from this poor, rural community because she always assumed they wouldn't be going to college. This incident illustrates as powerfully as any we have seen the value of using student and teacher data to change teachers' thinking and behavior. We must make sure that there is a nonjudgmental atmosphere in place when we review data so that teachers feel free to make public these aha moments.

When student and teacher perceptions of school climate are compared side by side, at least two scenarios are possible. First, if there is general agreement between students and teachers about a question, this offers evidence that people see the issues in a similar way. These results can reflect some schoolwide consensus about a particular question, issue, or practice. For example, for the question, "In our school, positive student behavior is recognized," 75 percent of students agreed, along with 79 percent of teachers. Here, it is pretty clear that some form of positive behavior supports system (OSEP, 2011) is being used within the school. Individuals might differ about how effective it is to reward students for positive behavior, but there would appear to be a general agreement that this practice is in use at this school.

But for another question, such as, "Our discipline system provides support for students to help them learn from their mistakes," 65 percent of teachers agree, along with just 17 percent of students. This indicates the need for some real dialogue about what these numbers might mean, and how the school's discipline practices may need rethinking. For many questions in almost every school, there's a distinct disparity between student and teacher perceptions. Differences like these can initiate some wonderful conversations about what is *really* happening in a school.

When data from one group seem to contradict responses from another group, some are led to question the data themselves. In one school, their survey results showed that 73 percent of teachers agreed with the statement,

"When adults take action to stop bullying it really works." Yet, just 24 percent of students agreed with the statement. As teachers reviewed their results, some were angry and questioned the data. Others found fault with the question or said, "How do students know if the system works, they're just kids!" But by talking through this divergence with colleagues, other insights can arise. A teacher might point out, "Maybe these kids see things we don't see. Maybe they see the students we punish for bullying turn right around and do it again and again, no matter how many detentions or in-school suspensions we give them!" Another teacher may observe, "How realistic is it to take any action to stop bullying after it occurs? Maybe we need to focus more on prevention than reaction?"

PREVENTING PITFALLS: RESOLVE DIVERGENT DATA

In almost every school we've studied, on several questions related to teaching and learning, student numbers predictably diverge widely from teachers. For example, almost 100 percent of teachers typically report they offer choices to students about class work, while typically less than 30 percent students will say they have these choices. The only way to resolve this apparent paradox is to talk to the students—and teachers. This is not an area of disagreement where teachers are saying they don't believe in offering choices, but their perception of choice obviously is much different from students. Why? Often in this case, it is a different perception of frequency—teachers report they offer choices of assignments a couple times a year; some students would like to see choices much more often. Or, teachers offer choices to some students or in some classes (typically for the "stronger" students) but not for others. All of this is interesting food for thought.

When comparative data on school climate don't match, showing that the perceptions of one group are fundamentally different from the perceptions of another, this can create the cognitive dissonance that generates rich discussion and exploration. We have found that with the proper facilitation and support, it is the conversations where teachers work collaboratively with students to resolve this cognitive dissonance that often yield the most potent school climate goals and action project ideas.

GOAL SETTING WITH STUDENT LEADERS

The issues raised by the data become the basis for goal setting with student leaders. To be constructive, we aim to have students restate problems as goals to be achieved. Thus, the issue of "unresponsive teaching" can be restated as a goal to "make teaching more responsive to individual student interests and learning needs." An issue of disrespect among students may be reworded as "increasing the percent of students who feel valued and respected by peers." We emphasize the need to cite specific data or evidence for each goal, which serves to legitimize the goal and act as a benchmark for measuring future progress. For example, a school might choose to set a goal "to increase responsive teaching." They might identify a 10 percent increase in positive student and teacher responses to questions about responsive teaching as evidence of progress.

We usually aim for one goal from the student group under each of the school climate standards. This number helps offer a reasonable scope for school improvement and begins to align student thinking with the national standards. In practical terms, the best action projects tend to address several standards simultaneously. For example, a student-led judiciary not only handles disciplinary issues but empowers students and improves relationships in school. It also reduces workload for teachers and administrators so they can spend more time on the educational purposes of school. Because action projects tend to touch multiple standards, strictly defining goal areas seems less essential than having the student team feel successful and efficient in identifying themes and setting overall direction for action.

To state what we think may be obvious, setting specific targets is important both to establish direction and goals and to make clear that incremental progress and growth is the real goal. No one is unrealistic about expecting perfection just around the corner. Is it reasonable to expect the school to go from 45 percent of the students feeling "excited about many of the things I am learning at school" to being 100 percent? Certainly not in one year, and maybe not ever. But, we can aim to improve by 10 percent or 20 percent this year, and build on these successes to make further progress in ensuing years. This can lead to greater credibility with stakeholders often jaded by the "fad of the month" promising more than it can deliver. Achieving reasonable goals builds capacity within the school for continuous and sustained improvement over time.

PREVENTING PITFALLS: AVOID SETTING TOO MANY GOALS

There is only so much any school can do well. Once a school starts looking seriously at data, there are countless areas for improvement. Choosing too many goals will overwhelm everyone and lead to frustration. What is so different about the collaborative action research approach is that it isn't a new initiative, but a means of building organizational capacity to continually improve schools—a few issues at a time. Positively addressing one issue usually has synergistic positive impact on other issues. And, there will always be other issues to address together in subsequent years.

WHY STUDENTS LEAD THE WAY: STUDENT AND TEACHER DATA ANALYSIS AND GOAL SETTING

The last step for the student team in this goal-setting meeting is to practice sharing their results with the faculty. This opportunity to speak in front of their teachers in itself sends a powerful message about leadership and student participation. Faculty meetings are this mysterious netherworld to most students, and being invited to participate can feel like being invited to a secret society.

The purposes of the student presentation to the faculty are as follows:

- Explain the data analysis and goal-setting process.
- Share the goals the students identified.
- Demonstrate the responsibility and support of the student leadership team.
- Inspire the faculty to take part in improving school climate and learning.

Putting students center stage—where they can explain how they analyzed the data in words and numbers and they can share their findings—achieves these goals. The students bring newsprint sheets with each of their goals articulated and supported by data from specific survey questions. These sheets serve as cue cards for the kids, visuals for the audience, and a model for teachers who will be asked to engage in the same analysis and goal-setting process immediately following the students' presentation.

Invariably, seeing their students step up in these leadership roles entrances the teachers and makes them receptive to almost anything the students say. This is an ideal opportunity for students to share some of the more critical perspectives emanating from the surveys. The quotes can serve to bring personal voice to otherwise sterile numbers. The main student presenter might share a numerical statistic, such as 36 percent of students agree that "I feel excited about many of the things I am learning in school." The impact of this number hits home when followed by another student reading the quote, "I don't see how anything I learn in school will help in my future," and a different student from the leadership team reciting, "I wish I didn't wake up every day dreading another day of nothing."

Using individual quotes from focus groups or surveys is a powerful strategy for touching the hearts, minds, and imagination of teachers, students, and administrators. Powerful words taken from the qualitative data can serve as a potent tool for lending urgency and building teacher engagement and commitment to the work of school climate improvement. For example, one student wrote,

What I love about this class is we get to make choices about the things we learn. My daddy is in Iraq and I worry about him all the time. I'm so thankful I got to learn more about where he is because my teacher let me do my social studies project on Iraq. I still learned a lot about the Middle East too.

If teachers listened carefully to the words of this student, how could they deny the value of providing students with choices in their classrooms?

PREVENTING PITFALLS: AVOID PUTTING TEACHERS ON THE DEFENSIVE

Quotes from students can be tremendously powerful when read aloud to teachers. Teaching students to read each quote as if it was theirs enhances the impact. Encourage students not to preface the quote with "one student said." We instruct the student leaders to just read it as if they wrote it, using first person language.

While quotes are intended to get teachers' attention, they shouldn't be off-putting and derail progress. It is recommended that the quotes are tied to numbers data to offer context. One student might state a goal area and cite survey statistics that define the issue. One or two students can then read quotes that illustrate the issue area.

To note, be sure to collect data summaries after meetings with students and teachers. Not that this is "top-secret" work—in fact, we hope the work is well publicized and transparent within the school—but we also know that some people can take information out of context to meet a personal agenda. These distortions, among people or in the press, can derail the positive work of the collaborative action research process.

When we begin the process of goal setting with teachers, we start by asking student leaders to each select two or three quotes from their review of the qualitative data. These quotes should represent their most significant concerns or positive qualities about their school. At the ensuing faculty meeting, the students line up in front of the room full of teachers and take turns reading the words of their peers aloud, just as if they wrote them. Again, qualitative data can reveal perspectives on school climate, respect, and learning that no number or statistic can communicate as effectively. These student quotes jumpstart the discussion among teachers about issues to focus on to improve school climate, student engagement, and learning.

Following the student presentation of their data analysis and goals, most teachers are ready to analyze the data themselves to confirm or dispute the student findings and to sit with colleagues to construct their own understandings. Because the students have already seen and interpreted the data through their lens, it is less likely that teachers can discount, dismiss, or deny the survey results. And, knowing that the students want to be part of the solution, the faculty realizes they have support and a resource for actually making positive change that has a reasonable chance of making a difference. (See Appendix C for a sample showing Student Goals and Evidence of Need.)

FACULTY DATA ANALYSIS AND GOAL SETTING

Students leave the room after they complete their brief presentation to the teachers. The faculty then carries out their own data analysis and goal-setting process. In the interest of time efficiency and to encourage cross-fertilization of ideas, the faculty is divided up randomly into table groups when they enter the room. Each table is assigned a particular standard and asked to analyze those data, both the numbers and words, and identify issues they feel are worth addressing related to this standard topic. If there are more table groups than standards, multiple tables can work with the same standard; this can serve as one more check on validity by comparing conclusions of different teacher groups in the school.

PREVENTING PITFALLS: DISCOURAGE TEACHERS FROM WORKING IN SELF-SELECTED GROUPS

The SafeMeasures process is meant to alter unproductive patterns in schools. This means breaking up groupings among teachers that may limit their openness to change. A simple method for this is for student leaders to give each teacher a numbered card or one with a picture that instructs where to sit. This random grouping mixes up teachers and allows them to hear different perspectives from a diverse group of colleagues.

Based on their review of the data, each table group writes their goal(s), with accompanying statistical support, on newsprint. When all the groups are ready, they each have a brief time to explain to the whole group the goals they identified from the data.

The final step in the goal-setting process is prioritizing from among all the goals the faculty and students generated. Posting all the newsprint around the room and giving every teacher five colored dots to allocate according to their own preferences allows quick ranking of the most widely valued goals from the entire group. The top three or four choices offer a good starting point for school change—diverse enough to impact various aspects of school life, but hopefully limited enough to keep things manageable and realistic.

After just an hour and a half, there is general agreement at the faculty meeting about data-based goals to improve school climate and learning. In almost every school we work with, this brings a palpable sense of accomplishment, a not small degree of surprise, and a refreshing feeling of enthusiasm for the work ahead. Optimism now prevails: There is a process in place that is efficient, effective, inclusive, and forward looking.

PREVENTING PITFALLS: AVOID OVERLY AMBITIOUS GOALS

Collaborative action research isn't a miracle process. Aiming to solve the most intractable problems as a first step may be too much to undertake right off. There is a reason why these problems are intractable—they are entrenched and hard to solve. Be realistic, then, about issues these leadership teams can address. In setting goals, state the benchmarks in terms of *improvement* rather than *solving*. It is much more realistic to aim to improve respect among students by 10 percent per year, for example, than to state a goal of eliminating disrespect among students.

THE WORK OF GOAL-BASED ACTION TEAMS

The final step of Stage Three is to form goal-based action teams to begin the action-planning process. Up to this point, groups have been formed randomly to analyze the schoolwide data. This step allows individuals to follow their interests and passions. Most people are much more committed to something they choose and something that resonates with their concerns, talents, interests, and expertise. Forcing an English teacher to help make the science program more hands-on will probably prove less meaningful to the teacher than working to create a communitywide reading forum.

With the three or four goals identified, we ask each teacher and student leader to choose a goal that they would most like to work on. This is one more chance to "vote with your feet" on the relative importance of each goal. If no one goes to a particular goal group, this provides a pretty clear message showing that goal is not a current priority for this group.

These goal-based action teams will be charged with the most crucial step of developing and implementing action plans to address the goal for their team. As these action teams are formed, the initial steps are to evaluate the team's composition and make a plan for working together. How many people are in the group? What about this issue area led them to choose this team? What are their initial ideas on ways to address this goal? What inspires them at this moment about working on this issue? What is their vision of results if this group is successful addressing this goal?

PREVENTING PITFALLS: AVOID JUMPING TO A SOLUTION

At this stage, the purpose is to generate a wide range of ideas and perspectives. Ultimately, a school will need multiple action projects to address this issue area for everyone in the school. Make sure to record the whole range of this initial thinking—it will save time later and generate a starting list of ideas. The real work of change is in the action projects; thinking creatively about these can be daunting, but also incredibly inspiring.

This is a time full of opportunity and possibility—enjoy the success of reaching this point and prepare for the adventure of effecting real change.

MAKING IT REAL: DATA ANALYSIS AND GOAL SETTING WITH CHAIN REACTION

Chain Reaction (CR), an elementary school student leadership team from New Hampshire, began the process of data analysis while they were still conducting their surveys. One student leader named Maya excitedly asked her adult mentor, "When will we get a chance to see what everybody said?" Students are always being asked to complete surveys, but in our experience, they very seldom ever see the results. Maya was curious and eager to learn what everybody had said about their school.

The numbers group learned how to read the data summary, seeing that "big numbers" (percentage of positive responses) were good, and "small numbers" were not so good. We showed them how to compare teacher and student responses on each item, which they found fascinating. They also compared responses of boys and girls, white and nonwhite students, and college-bound and noncollege-bound students. They were amazed when they found some differences as large 60 percent or 70 percent in the responses of different groups.

While the words group was selecting quotes and practicing presenting these, the numbers group made posters showing the evidence from their survey data they felt were most important. The number groups presented their key findings to the rest of the CR team and then each student was given four sticky dots for voting. They each placed a dot next to the survey items listed on the posters that they thought were most significant. The team counted the dots and chose those items that had the most votes as the key issues the CR team would work to address.

The four most important items identified by the CR team through this dot-voting process were these:

1. When adults try to stop bullying, it really works.	Students 46%	Faculty 68%
2. I often hear students make hurtful comments or jokes about other students.	Students 66%	Faculty 32%
3. Students in my school try to help when they see someone being bullied.	Students 66%	Faculty 35%
4. I feel safe on the bus.	Students 57%	Not asked

One of the students from the words group said, "Hey, the quote I picked says the same thing!" She read aloud to the CR team:

My little brother keeps getting bullied and sweared at on bus #97. He told his teacher, but it doesn't stop. He told the bus driver and she never does anything to stop it. He doesn't want to come to school anymore. I am worried about my brother; somebody needs to help him.

The CR team chose bullying as the problem they wanted to work on. They set three goals to address the problem:

1. Work with teachers to help make the playground and bus a safer place for everyone.
2. Help teachers understand the places in school where bullying takes place so that teachers can help stop it.
3. Create a way students could stand up to bullies and get help when they need it.

After the Chain Reaction team had completed their data analysis and goal setting, they were ready to help their teachers do the same. The student leaders met with teachers after school. The words group sent some emotional shock waves through the room as they recited fifteen quotes from the students' qualitative data to their teachers. "Each of these quotes represents only one student," said Maya, "but each one is important for us all to hear."

Then the numbers group shared the student and teacher school climate survey results with their teachers. The student leaders explained how their teachers could analyze the data summary just as they had already done. They showed teachers how to use the dots to vote for the key issues that they thought the school should work to address.

When the teachers completed their process and the CR team showed them their goals, the teachers realized they had seen many of the same things in the data, and that both groups wanted to do a better job with bullying. Teachers told the CR team that they had also chosen to work on the more general issues of respect and respectful teaching. The teachers were committed to working with the CR team to try to deepen student engagement in learning as a way to improve school climate and learning at their school.

As the school year ended, to cap off their first year as a leadership team, the CR team attended the governor's signing of the new anti-bullying law with students from across the state. The school now has a specific focus for improving school climate and learning. The school will continue to work together to develop action plans and projects to address their goals, and deal more effectively with bullying and making learning more engaging for all students.

CONCLUSION

There usually is great energy when students and teachers sit down to analyze the data. Students are eager to find out what their peers and teachers had to say about their school. When students present their findings and goals to the teachers, they demonstrate the fact that they are willing to step up and take responsibility to improve their schools. In our experiences, this often brings out the best in teachers and school leaders. They willingly work together to follow the students' spirited example. They are ready to take on the challenge of developing action projects to effect changes in school climate that will enable them to meet their newly set goals.

SIMPLE SUMMARY: STAGE THREE

- Be sure to review qualitative data and ensure that individuals are not personally identified (remove any names or personal references).
- Set up a meeting with principal and adult design team to review data before meetings with students and faculty.
- Share qualitative (words, quotes) and quantitative (statistics) results with principal, adult design team, and student leadership team.
- Have student leadership team divide into two groups to analyze the qualitative and quantitative data (a words group and a numbers group, depending upon their interests).
- Have the SLT numbers group identify three of the most powerful school climate improvement "needs/problems" that they see in the quantitative data.
- Have the SLT words group identify a set of twelve to fifteen of the most powerful quotes from the qualitative data that reflect important issues that they want their teachers to hear.
- Create a plan with adult design team leaders and principal for presenting any difficult data to faculty and students.
- Invite student leaders to present school climate data to faculty. To open the faculty meeting, students from the words team present their data by reading powerful quotes that they feel represent important problems.

- Have students from the numbers team invite their teachers to review the school climate data and set three goals—as the SLT has done—based on their understanding of the most important school climate needs or problems shown by the data.
- Obtain a faculty commitment to work with the adult design team and student leadership team on the next stage—to develop interventions to address these problems and reach their respective school climate goals.

BOOK STUDY QUESTIONS

1. Choose five to ten questions you would most like to ask students about their school experience. Turn these into a survey, as statements each student can rate as strongly agree, agree, neutral, disagree, or strongly disagree. Add a qualitative, open-ended question at the end of the survey, such as, "Is there anything else you would like to share with us about your school and how well it is working for you?" Ask one class to complete this survey as you administer the process. Ask another class to complete the survey with a student administering. Ask a few teacher colleagues to answer the same survey.

2. Analyze the survey data by adding together all the positive responses for students and teachers. Compare results. What are areas where students and teachers are similar in perceptions? What are areas where their perceptions differ? What might explain these differences?

3. Are there questions where the scores are particularly low or particularly high? What is your response to these high or low scores?

4. Look at answers to the open-ended question. How do these words from the students add to the survey numbers?

5. Are there differences in responses when teachers administered the survey compared to when a fellow student administered it? What can you learn from this about who should be involved in data collection?

6

Stage Four: Making Change Happen

Action Planning and Project Development

Begin somewhere; you cannot build a reputation on what you intend to do.

Liz Smith (n.d.)

MAYBE WE SHOULD ASK THE KIDS:
REFLECTIONS OF A DESIGN TEAM MEMBER

It seemed a little surprising that teachers and students chose such similar goals for school improvement, but maybe the kids really are more serious about school than some teachers had thought. Admittedly, these goals related to challenges the school had faced for years—lack of respect, unmotivated kids, poor academic performance. We'd tried everything; what could be different this time?

I guess the one difference right off was that there were kids around the table with teachers, together looking at these problems. We broke into teams to look at each goal, and it was nice to see teachers in the academic excellence group immediately talk about solutions (in contrast to so many meetings where we tend to lament the various struggles of our jobs and the weaknesses of "kids these days"). In maybe ten minutes, we adults came up with a bunch of, what I thought, were pretty good ideas. Then Terry, the always thoughtful American history teacher, noted we have a couple students here and maybe we should ask them for their ideas.

It was a bit deflating to hear these students nix most of our ideas. We're the "professionals" and usually feel like we know best. But the kids were probably right that our solutions were really just the latest version of teachers "doing school to kids"—more rewards for the strongest students, harsher consequences for inadequate schoolwork, more PR about the long-term benefits of learning.

The kids were diplomatic in proposing a different approach. How about more choice for students in classes to pick topics to study, or formats to present their work? Maybe a committee of students and teachers could look at curriculum together to find ways to inspire all kids? And, that idea for Project Week those consultants explained seemed about the coolest thing we could do that last week of the school year to let every student follow their interests to show what they can do.

Over the next few weeks, these ideas blossomed into full-fledged plans. Best of all, most of the work was done by the students, who were tremendously motivated to make sure this worked. They recruited their peers and promoted their ideas. The students' strategy to talk to each teacher individually made it almost impossible for any teacher to turn them down, especially with the specific suggestions the kids made for each class.

In the short-term, I don't know how much really changed in any particular class. I was more conscientious about offering choices more frequently. The curriculum group is meeting but they won't have anything to report for a while. And Project Week is still months off. But there is a different feel in school—kids seem more upbeat, teachers are asking kids how classes are working, there is a sense we are working together.

Just last week, a usually disengaged student came to me after class and asked if, instead of my assignment to write a short paper on the 1960s, could he make a video instead? This would be a lot more work, I told him, but he was undaunted. His "video essay" was about the most insightful presentation of the contrasts between the hippie culture and more traditional American life of that period that I have seen in twenty years of teaching this topic. Not bad.

ACTION PLANNING: WHERE CHANGE BEGINS

In any organization, it is much easier to discuss an idea into the ground than to actually take action. Studying an issue, assigning an idea to committee, and discussing different viewpoints are safe and noncontroversial. No particular commitments are necessary and if nothing is tried, there is no risk of failure.

Neither schools as institutions nor most individuals have the time or energy to devote to discussions that go nowhere. In the end, deeds mean more than words. Simply showing the effort to improve school climate sometimes does as much to impact relationships among teachers and students as any particular action. Positive school climate is about demonstrating, through actions, that each child matters, that learning is about engaging experiences, and that positive relationships are central to the smooth functioning of schools.

Implementation of action creates energy, inspires commitment, and motivates further action. This is what leads to meaningful and sustained change in schools. Making something happen allows people to feel like their time was well spent, that they are making a difference, that they are part of a real movement to make change—that they have the power to make a difference for themselves and for the school as a whole.

NO ONE BEST SYSTEM

Many of us are familiar with schools searching for the perfect action in response to an issue. With limited capacity, energy, time, and money, no one wants to devote resources to some action that has limited chance for success. (At the same time, many who work in schools have well-grounded skepticism based on years of failed reforms, "faddish" ideas, or new programs that take loads of energy with little real results for teachers or students.)

In our work with the SafeMeasures™ process, we have learned that there rarely is one best solution, that how efforts are processed often means more than the particular action taken, and that no one action is ever going to be the silver bullet to achieve the results we seek.

We recommend a set of paradigm shifts that result in real and sustained change in school climate and culture:

- *The energy and resources in schools are finite when we rely exclusively on the adults working in schools.* By including students as leaders, we vastly expand the resources available to apply to action planning.
- *Kids know best (or at least are worth listening to).* Adults in schools can spend hours coming up with ideas they think might be effective. Including students in this conversation almost always results in better ideas.
- *Actions should be related directly to needs.* Too often, schools jump at a new program that sounds good or is convenient without first identifying the problem they are seeking to address. The SafeMeasures process starts with school climate data to identify goals that then lead to action projects.
- *Stop looking for the "one right way."* What works for one person may not work for another. A combination of small and larger actions tend

to be more effective in reaching more students and teachers, generating ongoing energy for change, and developing the culture in schools where adults and kids work together to continually improve school climate.

- *Remember the three tiers of students.* Basing schoolwide practices on the most needy 5 percent can be oppressive for the majority. Likewise, thinking what works for the vast majority should work for all is equally unrealistic. Reducing disrespect is much different from developing respect. Focusing on the respect side of the continuum leads to sustained change; personalization, relationships, and empowerment serve as building blocks to even greater respect.

These are the lessons of this chapter on action planning—jump into action, work with those ready to "play along," pilot new ideas, modify as you go, work with good will, and keep looking for ways to *enhance, extend,* and *expand* action.

SCHOOL CLIMATE ACTION TEAMS: WORKING EFFECTIVELY WITH COLLEAGUES

We know that every individual has different passions and interests. Too often in schools we expect every teacher to be equally committed and involved in whatever effort the school is undertaking. But teachers are at different places in their careers, have different family or personal needs, or simply have more or less affinity for a particular idea. If we expect everyone to be equally involved in every program, we undoubtedly will be disappointed.

In some schools, where there is an enthusiastic group of teachers dedicated to improving climate and others less ready for this, we often recommend focusing on those "ready to play." It is easier to harness the energy of supporters than to try to convince, cajole, or coerce those with less interest. Positive energy and positive results often do more to generate support and involvement than working to change people's minds before moving forward.

When possible, it is ideal to include everyone in school climate improvement. But even if everyone supports this general commitment to acting on school climate, there will surely be differences in what each adult finds most motivating. As a first step, it is recommended that teachers form goal area teams based on personal preference. Let those most concerned with discipline work on discipline; let ones more disposed to celebrating successes and honoring individual student accomplishments focus on this. By operating on several fronts, change becomes more systemic and can weave varied efforts into a more coherent whole.

PREVENTING PITFALLS: AVOID FORCING COMMITMENT

Sometimes it is best to work with those ready to play. There are always naysayers, some who may have good reasons to limit their involvement due to having other personal or work related commitments. Voice and choice are essential to getting beyond compliance to promote engagement. This is true for students in school as well as faculty in their work. Allowing individuals to choose their goal team and level of involvement taps into positive energy.

Even within goal teams, some faculty will be more big-picture types and others more detail oriented. Some are more into trying something new, others on building upon past practices. This is all good! We want to tap into individual strengths, not force individuals into uncomfortable positions.

ACTION PLANNING STEPS

To frame the action planning stage, we ask groups to answer three questions:

- What are you currently doing related to this goal?
- What new ideas can you brainstorm that might address this goal?
- What activities from the Action Planning Ideas (see Figure 6.1) seem worth looking into to address this goal in your school?

The first question honors the work already going on at the school. Almost every school has some programs and practices aimed at creating a positive school climate. SafeMeasures isn't intended to tell schools they are failing—instead, it helps schools identify areas they want to improve, regardless of all the positive efforts already in place. It is important to recognize the work already underway—building on what is working and abandoning what isn't. For example, a school may have scheduled advisory time, and this can offer a perfect platform to build better relations among students and faculty.

The second question taps into the talents of teachers and students to imagine something new. Unleashing the creativity and passions of teachers and students is inspiring—it is amazing how individuals empowered to implement their own ideas will devote the time and energy to assure they work. One school made each teacher a "guru" responsible for one small area of school well-being—the young teacher who chose to head up "social affairs" initiated birthday recognitions for all students and helped start an outdoor club, while she expanded her own leadership skills; another teacher led a tech club that helped with repairs of school computers.

Figure 6.1   Action Planning Ideas

Goal Area: Respect Among Students			
Respect Continuum Focus	*Small Project Ideas*	*Medium Project Ideas*	*Large Project Ideas*
Relationships	• Include more activities to introduce students to peers. • Encourage students to hang out or eat lunch with student they don't know. • Hang posters around school relating to diversity and respect. • Select a school theme or slogan focused on improving respect.	• Designate special behavior days/weeks (e.g., Thank-Others Day, Random-Acts-of-Kindness Week). • Hold outside-of-class, all-school (or all-grade) events such as Mountain Day or College Visit Day.	• Collect data on relationships and use to measure weekly or monthly progress. • Take on a project where students find and communicate with a sister school in an impoverished or otherwise quite different environment. Have students study the culture and geography of the area, and initiate weekly Skype or other web-based meetings with students at that school. This could lead to exchange visits between schools.
Engaged Learning	• Bring in inspiring outside presenters. Then establish a regular meeting by Skype or other web-based mechanism to keep the connection alive and vibrant. • Discuss gender and race issues in specific classes (health, social studies, etc.).	• Ask students for their suggestions on parts of films or music that pertain to what they are studying. Use these in class whenever possible. • Incorporate multiple intelligence (MI) and differentiated teaching. • Encourage independent study opportunities. • Have students engage in community service. • Have each class select a project to work on, such as reading a common book around school theme.	• Organize Project Week with regular classes replaced by individual or group projects that value diverse skills and interests. • Hold Culture Days. • Incorporate collaborative service learning or problem-based learning.

Respect Continuum Focus	Small Project Ideas	Medium Project Ideas	Large Project Ideas
		• Ask students for help in identifying and recruiting appropriate guest speakers, or in locating websites that add depth to course material.	
Personalization	• Create student-led welcome team for new students at beginning of school year. • Celebrate student work on bulletin boards. • Recognize students of the month (or week) in many classes.	• Organize all-class/all-school fun team game related to diverse talents. • Hold talent show–type events that recognize and encourage diverse talents beyond sports and academics—especially if these programs raise self-respect levels of most students by identifying students' strengths. (Be careful not to leave certain kinds/groups of students out.) • Build personal connections between students by creating peer buddies across grades and having cross-grade classes or activities. • Create student help team that looks out for new students and also for kids who may be having a "downtime." • Create student activity fund to help students pursue options.	• Assign a backpack project to give each new student a "survival kit" for school. • With permission from students, copy and bind their best work and have it available in the school's library. • Showcase senior and junior projects. • Encourage student-led and independent classes and exploratories. • Increase understanding of issues of diversity, tolerance, acceptance, and respect via thorough attention in classes, curriculum, school events, and out of school experiences. • Create an advisory program. • Hold talent festivals (art fair, science fair, allied arts exhibits, etc.). • Hold all-school/class meetings with time for commendations. • Hold an official Giving Day.

(Continued)

Figure 6.1   (Continued)

Respect Continuum Focus	Small Project Ideas	Medium Project Ideas	Large Project Ideas
Empowerment	• Have students take turns on intercom announcements. • Conduct a focus group, run by students, to discuss what are the respect issues at this school.	• Use focus group data to form small teams and hold additional meetings on each specific issue (e.g., girls' treatment of girls; boys' treatment of girls; why would someone want to be a Goth? What does special education really mean?). • Have the student leadership group identify the "hot spot" areas where behavior is worst (bathrooms? lunchroom? bus? gym?). Discuss how to create a monitoring system at these locations, or other mechanisms to promote positive behavior in these locales.	• Have a group of existing students run orientation for new students. • Create a student judiciary—peer mediation group that handles referred cases dealing with student-student conflicts. • Train students as peer helpers or mediators who can take the lead in challenging hateful language, harassment, and bullying.

The last question asks goal teams to draw on best practices that have proven successful elsewhere. Sadly, with their busy schedules, very few teachers have the chance to see many of the great practices going on elsewhere (even in the same building or district). Figure 6.1, the Action Planning Ideas, provides a treasure trove of tested ideas organized around specific goals.

Many of the best action projects turn out to be "two-fers"—addressing two (or more) goals with one structure. For example, Project Week (where each student proposes and completes an individual learning project of their own choosing) is a structure to make learning more engaging while increasing student choice, developing independent learners, and celebrating individual talents and interests. While few of us experienced these best practices when we went to school, these are fundamental structures in many schools that produce the most robust results in studies of school climate and academic performance.

Figure 6.1 lists projects within each goal area organized by placement on the Respect Continuum and project size, and shows a small part of an action planning guide for one goal. Note that some projects easily can fit in more than one goal area—in fact, the best ideas hit multiple goals. (A more complete guide is available from Main Street Academix, www .msanh.com.)

USING THE RESPECT CONTINUUM AS A GUIDE TO ACTION

The Respect Continuum can help schools determine their immediate focus, and also serve as the route to long-term change. Having determined goals in Stage Three, tied directly to evidence from the SafeMeasures surveys, the Respect Continuum can help target which kinds of actions fit best with the school culture and will move the school forward in a reasoned manner.

Vygotsky's (1978) concept of the "zone of proximal development" applies as much to school improvement as it does to student learning. Just as a beginning writer is not asked to suddenly write a novel, we shouldn't expect a school with few strong relationships between teachers and students to jump into empowering kids as the best next step.

The Respect Continuum serves more as a framework than a delineated path. It is not always the case that empowerment is superior to personalization, or that before engaged learning can occur more positive relationships must develop. In actual practice, the lines between the levels of the continuum are blurry and fluid. Relationships between teachers and students improve through engaged learning. When learning is more personalized, students feel empowered and more engaged. But our experience is that there is a general flow along this continuum that can provide guideposts for change and greater specificity in planning action projects.

PREVENTING PITFALLS: PROMOTE CONSISTENCY

When schools concentrate on only one area of change, especially with larger high schools, the disjunction between the supportive, respectful actions in one area and less respectful practices elsewhere can be seen as more hypocritical than hopeful. While it is impossible to address every issue in school at once, climate is about the overall life in school. Aim to be as comprehensive as possible—with multiple action projects across various aspects and programs of schools that can send a clear and visible message to all in the school that "this time, things are different."

MOVING TOWARD THE POSITIVE

Many schools are so focused on the disrespect side of the continuum that their first steps probably have to begin with developing more positive relationships between teachers and students. Although most teachers enter the profession with a strong belief in the potential of every child, there is no shortage of reasons why this can change over time to a less positive orientation toward "those kids." Bad behavior, late homework, incomplete assignments, lack of parental support, overwhelming demands from state and federal bureaucracies—all can lead teachers to distance themselves from at least some students. Likewise, students can feel that school rules, teacher expectations, and the various demands of the system make them feel like powerless and anonymous pawns, subject to the authority of adults who control their lives in school.

This lack of belief in the goodness of others is no basis for positive school climate. When adults distrust students, they establish policies that students find increasingly confining and confrontational. Our local, small-town high school just wrestled through a debate about alcohol testing every student at the prom. Even the top students found this offensive, as one said, "It's insulting to spend all the time and money to look like a princess and then be treated like a criminal." Her classmate concurred, "If the administration wants respect, then it's a two-way street. You can't infringe on students' rights and expect them to respect you the next day." Although schools must provide a safe and orderly environment, if this is achieved only through imposing adult authority, students may comply with rules but have trouble developing the self-motivation, self-responsibility, and desire for doing their best in a school where they feel controlled by adults.

In contrast, focusing on the respect side of the continuum creates the conditions in which there are less incidents needing discipline. The positive climate helps each student feel valued and worthy of aiming for high achievement and positive contributions to the school and community.

A good first step toward respect in schools is developing relationships among teachers and students. Finding ways to humanize the environment, to get to know each other in varied contexts, to see that everyone has strengths and shortcomings, and to simply learn each other's names is a start to better relations.

RESPECTFUL TEACHING

Even friendly relations in the hallways won't mean much when the vast majority of student time is spent in classrooms where students feel they are just going through the motions of a boring and static curriculum. Respectful schools are characterized by respectful teaching—classes that students find engaging, purposeful, and meaningful. When the students feel learning experiences are designed with their success in mind, they feel more respected and are therefore more respectful and more motivated in their work. This, in turn, builds deeper teacher-student relationships fostered through academic work, rather than solely through personal relationships developed outside the learning goals of school.

Respectful teaching can go beyond interesting and active learning experiences as teachers learn how to personalize learning. Attention to differentiation and student choice can provide the kinds of challenge and support to help every learner succeed. While attending to state standards and desired learning results, assignments can be modified to align products or topics or processes with the needs and interests of individual students.

PERSONALIZING ASSIGNMENTS

When studying the human body, middle schoolers were invited to teach this material at the local elementary school for the fourth-grade class. The middle schoolers had to learn all the same information about the body as in a more "follow the textbook" approach, but were allowed to decide how to teach this to younger students, all with the real purpose of helping the elementary school that most had attended just a few years previously.

This personalization leads naturally to more empowered students (and teachers) who feel they have greater input into and control over the quality of their school experiences. As students are engaged in learning and respond to personalized learning opportunities, they demonstrate their talents and celebrate their interests. It is empowering for students to feel the learning process is responsive to their needs, and this can be extended through various opportunities to include students in the overall functioning of the school. Students are instrumental for giving feedback on the quality of learning and teaching, helping plan for school improvement, being part of school safety and discipline, and developing policies and practices that are likely to be truly effective in achieving the best results for all in the school community.

While this kind of empowerment can be a long stretch from how things currently work in some schools, proceeding along the steps of the Respect Continuum can be a vision for a respectful school that works for all. But, each school has to begin where they are—for many, starting simply on more positive relations may be the first step. Schools that already have friendly relations among adults and kids may choose to look more closely at the quality of classroom learning experiences for students. Many schools have been working on learning how to differentiate learning, and considering how to incorporate more student choice and personalized learning can enhance this. Or, some respectful teaching may be prevalent in one area of the school but could be extended across more courses in the school. We try to build on current efforts in each individual school, pushing to the next level to make a difference in overall school climate.

BALANCED LEADERSHIP: ADULTS AND STUDENTS JOINING FORCES FOR CHANGE

At one time in SafeMeasures, we organized action planning separately with students and teachers, allowing each to explore their best ideas that could then be coordinated (we hoped) into one cohesive plan. This can work, but we have learned it is more effective to bring students and teachers together in action planning right from the start. This is valuable for numerous reasons:

- *Time is a finite resource.* Neither adults nor kids in schools have endless time to meet. Likewise, adding steps to the process by meeting separately and then meeting together simply delays action that needs to start as quickly as possible. Meeting together streamlines the speed of the action planning process.
- *Students serve as "whine preventers."* There undoubtedly is much in schools that is frustrating to teachers. Complaining about these challenges rarely results in positive action. Having students at the table with adults seems to limit these complaints while focusing work for the adults who hope to model effective work practices for youth.
- *Students know what works.* In goal groups, teachers tend to jump right into solution ideas. After about five minutes, one of the adults in the group will realize they have an expert in their midst and turn to the student(s) to respond to these adult generated ideas. Kids know what is likely to work and what will not. Including students in the front end of planning leads to better results.
- *Ownership matters.* Everyone is more committed to policies and practices to which they feel connected. When adults and youth work together from the beginning on action planning (as well as previous stages of SafeMeasures) this develops leadership and ownership that motivates, engages, and inspires all to make the process work.

The format for bringing student and teacher leaders together involves forming goal teams based on individual interest. Goal teams tend to include somewhere between five and fifteen people, with at least one student on each team. The aim of the goal teams is to choose action projects to undertake that they believe will have the "most bang for the buck"—projects that are likely to make a real difference in improving results around the identified goal (in addition to improving other climate factors if possible). Knowing no single approach rarely works for all students or adults in a school, we direct each goal team to identify two or three projects on which to begin work, recommending one of these is small and one somewhat bigger.

The size of projects relates to either time frame or scope or both. A small project might be a poster campaign or school assembly to raise awareness around a goal such as building better relationships among peers and teachers. It is unlikely this kind of publicity will do much to create deeper relations, but it can build momentum for the goal team to feel a sense of accomplishment while raising awareness schoolwide that this is an issue worth addressing.

A bigger project may take more time to organize and implement, but will be more ambitious in scope and intended impact. For example, this might mean creating Mountain Day to let kids and adults share a challenging community experience outside the academic setting. A school in Maine tried out Periods of Discovery, where each adult in school leads a group exploring a passion that adult has outside their normal school role (e.g., teaching knitting or car repair or playing rock music). These all-school activities take greater commitment, but done well, these projects can engage every student and adult in getting to know each other better. They can also lead to other efforts to expand and extend these relations and the associated learning.

There are medium-range projects that are worth pursuing as well. These have a high chance of coming to fruition and can help maintain momentum for other leadership team plans targeting school climate improvement. Perhaps the goal team will decide to extend student of the month awards to include more students each month, or change this to student of the week, or include students in nominating awardees rather than just teachers. Or, some leadership teams decide to select teachers of the month in addition to students, or recognize students in each classroom rather than schoolwide. These middle-level projects often build on existing efforts and supplement other action projects to make this goal area a schoolwide focus.

MAKING IT REAL: THE BACKPACK PROJECT

Set in a classic old two-story brick building, Woodsville High School (WHS) is a regional school that brings together students from six small middle and elementary schools in the region, and forms a school district that spans hundreds of square miles of New Hampshire countryside. Woodsville students tell us that many incoming ninth graders have long had feelings of trepidation about moving from their tiny, local schools to the big, intimidating high school.

A variety of data from the past few years showed that the vast majority of discipline and academic problems were happening with ninth graders. Having identified this concern with the transition for incoming ninth graders, the student leadership team came up with a promising solution. In attempting to establish the tone for a stronger school community, the student leadership team wanted to try to make every new student feel welcome from the very beginning of their school experience at WHS.

Going beyond the simple measures of an opening day assembly or even a day of orientation, the leadership team decided to create back-to-school backpacks that they would hand deliver to every new student. Along with this was an invitation to a fun barbeque night with teachers and students before school started. This would allow people to begin to get to know each other outside school.

Each backpack included what the student leaders determined as critical supplies for high school—pens and paper, a planning calendar, a stress ball, and a first-year student survival guide. For the barbeque, the teachers agreed to wear shorts as the student leadership team requested. Although attire seems like a small thing, the students felt that seeing the teachers dressed casually might make them a bit more "human" for the new students. Watching teachers play silly games and compete against students and one another for fabulous prizes at the barbeque also added to the climate of comfort and fun. The student leadership team's home visits, the cool new backpack, and the personal invitation to the barbeque to meet teachers truly made each child feel welcome in their new high school.

While this was just a small part of the efforts to improve school climate at Woodsville, this backpack project set a tone that each individual mattered, that relationships were valued, and that people would literally go the extra mile to make each student feel welcome. This never could have been accomplished by teachers alone (nor is it likely teachers would even have thought of the idea)—it was the students who made this happen, and it was students who kept this positive energy rolling with subsequent projects such as a new peer tutoring system; a student sponsored event; and many trips to the middle and elementary schools, where the older students led activities to build trust and peer relationships that would make the high school seem less daunting in the future.

The results for Woodsville have been very positive. School climate has improved dramatically, student discipline problems among the first-year students dropped precipitously, and the student dropout rate has lowered. Now, Woodsville is turning its attention to changes in the classroom that will reinforce these projects.

Source: Bob Jones, Principal, Woodsville High School, Woodsville, NH.

CONCLUSION

There is no one right way, no perfect action project, that will transform a school. But a set of different approaches—some small, some more ambitious—can start the ball rolling. This array of action projects can begin a school's journey toward changing school practices and improving school climate and learning. Reaching this stage is important because during action planning, each teacher and student leader makes a commitment to *do something*. This sends a message to the whole school community that the real work of building a safer, more respectful and effective school has begun.

SIMPLE SUMMARY: STAGE FOUR

Stage Four begins with the SLT being led through the action planning process first, and then they help lead their teachers through the same process.

- Have SLT determine issue/goal. What is the issue or goal that your team will be working on? What is the evidence of need for working on this goal (e.g., survey data)?
- Identify target audience. Who will be your target audience for this project? Based on your data, your plan may only need to target a small population of your students and/or teachers.
- Raise awareness. How will you raise awareness of the issue and what your team is planning?
- Generate interest and engagement. What strategies are included in your plan for generating interest in what you are doing and engaging students and teachers in this project?
- Identify first project. What is the first project that you will begin working on? From your list of project ideas, pick one short, medium, or long-term project on which you will begin your work.
- Determine process for evaluating success. How will you know if your project worked? What will you use to evaluate your success?
- Incorporate empowerment and shifting power relations. How will your project empower students and teachers in your school? Does this project represent a shift in power relations in your school?

Once the SLT has completed their action plans, they then meet with teachers and repeat the preceding process with one SLT or DT member per table group as they begin the process with their teachers.

- Have each table work on one goal or need area to brainstorm strategies and ideas.
- Ask teachers these questions to avoid new "layers" of initiatives: What are we already doing to address this need that is working? What are we already doing to address this need that may need changing or fixing? What new ideas can we find to address these problems?
- Decide to shift or "tweak" power relations within each strategy to avoid "predictable failure." (Include choices, voice, empowering roles, real audiences, authentic, real-world tasks.)

(Continued)

(Continued)

- Choose small, quick projects to begin with (pilot projects with the willing), then move toward more complex or larger projects that involve more students and teachers.
- Assign specific roles and time frames to individuals to ensure someone is responsible for taking action.
- Make projects fun, engaging, personalized, and as public as possible.
- Ask SLT students to give adults feedback on their project ideas and plans, and codesign them with students whenever possible.
- Make sure that projects involve teachers and students inside classrooms, and connect to curriculum, instruction, and assessment practices whenever possible.

BOOK STUDY QUESTIONS

1. What is your school currently doing that directly addresses the quality of school climate?

2. Where are your efforts focused on the Respect Continuum? How much attention is aimed at limiting disrespect? How much on promoting respect?

3. How might more attention to the positive side of the Respect Continuum affect school climate and learning in your setting?

4. How does what occurs in classes support or undermine positive school climate?

5. What are students' perspectives on school climate and learning? Would they describe your school as a respectful environment? Would they describe classrooms as characterized by respectful teaching?

7

Stage Four Specifics

Action Projects to Promote Respectful Teaching and Learning

In my view, teaching is an intellectual and scientific profession, as well as a moral profession. That means that schools have to constantly process knowledge about what works and that teachers have to see themselves as scientists who continuously develop their intellectual and investigative effectiveness.

Michael Fullan, *Journal of Staff Development*
(as cited in Sparks, 2003, sec. 5, para. 4)

MAKING SCHOOL MATTER: MORE REFLECTIONS FROM DESIGN TEAM MEMBERS

Everyone knows the last week of the school year can be almost totally unproductive. We teachers are tired, the kids are ready for summer, it always seems way too hot, state tests are over, and we're all counting down the days until vacation. Although it was a big change to school tradition, our school climate leadership teams figured we didn't have much to lose by trying out Project Week for this typically wasted week.

In early May, we explained this idea to the students, and in advisory we coached our kids on planning individual projects they would be passionate about. The projects involving creative writing or a week as an artist were obviously "school friendly." "Can I do a project on motorcycles?" asked one student. Another wanted to hang out with a park ranger. And another wanted to do something with weight lifting. Maybe these were a stretch for "school," but as long as students could meet Project Week requirements for research, writing, and a final presentation, it seemed all these could work.

Fortunately, we had a few group project options from teachers that helped the kids not really ready to take on this level of independent work. A class on comedy, an outdoor club canoe trip, a technology group on computer building and maintenance, and a service project with the food shelter offered more concrete and preplanned options.

When the last week of school came upon us, classes were cancelled and the feeling of opportunity (and trepidation for many) was palpable throughout the school. Kids came to school, checked in with their Project Week mentor, and a messy whirl of work ensued.

The week turned out to be quite an eye opener. Many of the kids who struggled most in regular classes were Project Week stars. Researching evolving car technology, being blindfolded all week to learn about disability, or being in a sculptor's studio every day seemed to totally inspire these students who often seemed confined by regular classes. Some of our typically strongest students seemed a bit adrift without being assigned everything by a teacher. Would these kids be prepared for more independent life after high school if they were so teacher dependent during high school?

The Project Week "museum" in the gym at the end of the week was an upbeat way to end the year. The presentations illustrated such an impressive range of interests (and some hidden talents)! The work that students shared in that gym reflected a ton of more learning (and energy and pride) than what usually occurred in that last week (or most other weeks for that matter). And, I think we teachers learned more about our students and their potential. This gave us something to ponder over the summer regarding how we could expand on this kind of learning for the following year.

CHANGING SCHOOL CLIMATE THROUGH RESPECTFUL TEACHING

We know many schools start their school climate improvement efforts with smaller projects related to nonacademic areas. This typically includes behavior in the hallways, safety in bathrooms, or clarity about discipline. While this is a safe place to begin working on climate, the impact of these efforts is limited (although not insignificant—one high school in Tennessee that cleaned up their bathrooms, reduced problems in the parking lot, and added student hall monitors saw scores on their school climate assessment go up without direct attention to classroom issues).

Usually with several of the school goals identified in Stage Three, there is at least one that relates more directly to academic learning. Given that academics are a primary focus in school and take up the vast majority of student time, at some point it is essential to relate school climate to what happens in classrooms. If school climate work is separated from the academic arena, many teachers (and parents and students) will see it as nonessential. While it can help immensely to improve climate during passing periods, before and after school, and in "special" all-school events, the life of the school really depends greatly on life inside each and every classroom.

There are countless strategies for making learning engaging and meaningful for students. Unfortunately, very few teachers have the opportunity to visit other schools or classrooms to see what is possible beyond their own experience. In our work, we are lucky to be in loads of classrooms, witnessing brilliant teaching and inspired learning. This chapter aims to share some of these exceptional approaches for engaging students in more respectful learning—learning that builds relationships, personalizes instruction, and empowers students to strive for success.

Creating more engaged learning experiences invariably impacts school climate and student academic success. This is a natural "two-fer" where action projects can improve learning while also improving school climate. For example, portfolio roundtables lead students to reflect on their learning and growth, provide a forum for teachers to learn more about each student, and personalize assessment for each child. This can be a powerful structure to identify an individual student's strengths and areas for growth, for building deeper relations between teachers and students, and for viewing learning more holistically on an individual and schoolwide basis. Some of the more powerful and effective action projects for more engaged learning are explained in more detail in the following sections.

ENGAGEMENT STRATEGIES THAT WORK

Focusing on engaging students in learning reflects a level of respect for the learner. This alters the dynamic of school from something imposed on students to a recognition of the *inherent free will* of each individual to choose to participate (or not). Teachers and school leaders must understand that students, ultimately, do indeed have free will that can undermine even our best-laid plans.

Students can choose if they are going to listen to their teachers, do their homework, show up for school each day, or put energy into learning. No matter how much educators like to think that the adults are in charge when it comes to schooling, ultimately, it is each student who will choose to buy-in, think, and learn—*or not.* For schools to enlist a student's self-motivation, we need to think of school less as something done *to* or even *for* kids and more as something done in partnership *with* them.

Looking at dropout rates, acts of disobedience, noncompletion of school assignments, and other signs of student resistance in schools, it is clear that students have plenty of ways to exercise their capacity to confront or ignore school expectations. Even if some of this resistance has more to do with conditions outside the school than inside, we have found that when schools treat students with the respect of seeking to make learning engaging, meaningful, and worthwhile, discipline issues decrease while academic interest and quality rises.

Emerging research on the brain and learning is confirming what great educators have always known—that the brain "lights up" for complex, challenging, social, contextualized experiences. Learning is a natural process for our brains. The brain is wired to make connections, construct meaning, and solve problems. Our brains seek out patterns and want to interact in a social manner to develop understandings.

Too often, educational practices interfere with these processes natural to the brain, preventing the "flow" learners feel when they are truly engaged. The graveyard model of education, where students sit silently and motionless in rows, fights against the way our brain really works best. Denise Pope (2010) at Stanford University emphasizes the ABCs of engagement—*affective, behavioral,* and *cognitive* aspects of schoolwork that tie together to embrace students in the learning process. Neuroscience and our experience as teachers tell us that learning is maximized when experiences connect with students at an emotional level, actively involve them, and push student thinking.

Engaging students in learning doesn't require a complete overhaul of schools. Small changes, even done sporadically, can increase student ownership, interest, and motivation. In fact, we are not sure students would thrive if pushed into the most engaged learning experiences continuously. Most students love the chance to dive into challenging, complex, and intriguing student-centered projects at times, but they also can appreciate the chance to regroup periodically, work on more structured and concrete tasks, and be led by the teacher. It is not necessary for every learning activity to be grandiose and complex. But, we must do a better job of showing students respect by following their innate tendencies to pursue individual interests, make choices, express themselves, and make connections between their learning, their lives, and the world beyond the classroom walls. These strategies can help create more respectful classrooms and more respectful and effective schools.

Several factors seem crucial to realizing this vision for engaged learning: commitment to the success of every child, openness to questioning and challenging the traditions and "givens" about how schools should look and be organized, and the sharing of good examples and ideas that have proven effective in schools and classrooms. There are countless ways to enhance student engagement in learning. To trigger thinking, we next provide some of the more exciting ones we have seen.

Providing Students With Choices

Providing choice in courses or within a course of topic, process, or product is the most basic and common method of personalizing learning. Ideas for increasing choice include the following:

Assignment choices. Differentiate learning by allowing students to choose a topic to be studied or a product to be created. For example, students might choose to develop a written report about the 1960s, electing to study the civil rights, 60s music, art, or fashion. Whatever the topic, the students must exercise skills of research, critical thinking, organization, and writing. Alternatively, all science students could be required to study the topic of gravity, but allowed to choose how to present their understanding—a PowerPoint, a lab report, a narrated video, an essay, a creative writing story, or a cartoon. In each case, students must show they understand the science concepts and can communicate them accurately, regardless of the format.

Differentiation in the learning process. Allow students to work alone or in groups, follow a teacher-provided protocol, or create one of their own upon teacher approval. Give the students several assignments at one time and a due date for all of it together—help students determine how they each allocate time to complete all the work on their own schedule. Students can also be free to choose how much to value each assignment from this grouping (within established limits) to let them decide which is of most interest or importance to them. For example, in May, one school requires eleventh grade students to complete five different assessments of their skills—an SAT practice test, independent research project, independent reading, current events presentation, and a personal resume. Each student can weight their scores (before the assignments are graded and within a range prescribed by the teacher) to respond to the kind of work with which each student feels most skillful. Every student still does every assignment, but all students have an opportunity to reflect on their own strengths and interests in the manner time and energy are allocated.

Open invitation for suggestions. Offer students the chance to modify assignments. A standard last line in assignments can be: "If there is any part of this assignment you wish to change, please feel free to make a proposal to me." The teacher need not always agree to student proposals, but this both lessens their complaints (by putting the responsibility on them for suggesting better alternatives) and invites students to take responsibility for their learning needs. At times, students find ways to go far beyond what the teacher expects.

Mini-course electives. Include four- to eight-week intensive electives to break up the term and allow students to study a topic in greater depth, and also balance the breadth of required coursework. These can be a great chance to encourage cross-disciplinary thinking. For example: fast food and sustainability, oceans, filmmaking, Vietnam, or science of the mind.

Giving students choice does not mean giving up control. The teacher retains ultimate decision-making authority in the classroom. More important, by framing the choices, the teacher creates the parameters within which students can exercise their independence. The teacher doesn't say to the class, "Do whatever you want," or "Research some topic in U.S. history." Instead, the teacher may delineate that within the study of the 1940s, students must create a PowerPoint presentation on an issue of significance in World War II, but let each student choose the issue. Or the teacher may require all students to create a model of DNA, but allow them to choose materials (Rick's daughter actually knit a double helix for this assignment, while classmates made models with pipe cleaners, cereal pieces, erector sets, and even a thirty-foot-long paper mache monstrosity). Or, a teacher can stipulate that every student must investigate the topic of Steinbeck's writing, but allow any format a student chooses for a presentation.

The teacher's judgment is key to deciding when to allow a student to pursue an alternative option. A student who was a weak writer always asked if he could do anything but writing. Almost every time, I, Rick, would tell him he needed to practice his writing. Once in a while, when the higher-order thinking or content understanding I was after was more pressing, I might allow this boy to create a video or graphic model that could capture this depth of thought.

In our research in schools across the country, the *items on our survey relating to student choices nearly always receive the lowest number of positive responses.* Students report that they hardly ever have opportunities to make choices about the things they learn or how they learn. If there is one place that a school could begin to concentrate its leadership and attention to immediately and dramatically impact improving school climate and academic performance, our research suggests trying to implement some of the recommendations about student choice described here.

Authentic, Applied, Real-World Learning

Problem-based learning (PBL). Use PBL to challenge students with problems to solve rather than academic exercises to complete. While the distinction can be subtle, there is a palpable difference between the constrictions of a teacher generated assignment to "Write a two-page lab report on water testing following the directions below" and the excitement of "The school board is concerned about food safety in the cafeteria and asks this class to test our food and water, and then provide a report for them at their March meeting." PBL allows room for individual initiative in problem solving, approach, and decision making. By its nature, PBL demands higher-order thinking skills while students work with course concepts and content.

The most powerful learning experiences often involve students working on authentic, *real-world problems*. These problems give students a sense of purpose and a "client" who may benefit from their work. Real-world problems change the dynamic in the classroom from working merely for a grade to working for a purpose. The benefits are numerous, one of which is addressing the challenge of *transference*—helping students develop the ability to apply what they learn in school to situations outside school. Real problems are often "messy"—asking students to use what they learn in school on novel and complex problems that challenge their abilities and often require skills and knowledge that transcend the somewhat artificial subject distinctions we make in school.

One key to managing real problems for students is to develop a solid problem statement that connects course learning objectives to a community need. We often ask community partners for "back burner" issues—something they can't normally get done themselves or in their busy work schedule, making them less immediately dependent on the work of school-age children. As teachers, we can then build the problem statement around this need, and embed course content and learning goals within this problem. We try to make the problem open-ended enough for students to apply their own approaches and skills in solving it, but with enough direction to assure they use their classroom learning in their work (see Figure 7.1).

Authentic, real-world problems. Consider beginning with some of the "generic" problems that can work with almost any community partner— evaluating how their organization is perceived in the community, creating a report on what other similar organizations are doing elsewhere in the country, assessing how the needs for their services might change in the future, or surveying clients of the organization about their satisfaction with services. These are real needs for almost every nonprofit, which usually are too immersed in the daily delivery of services to be able to reflect on their work and the bigger picture. Within these problems, it is easy to create a focus on elements most related to a particular course. For example, the teacher can ask the students to report on how new research in science might affect the needs of a low-income population being served, or to do an environmental impact statement on the organization's work, or to do a cost and quality analysis on services currently offered. This kind of reporting can be tremendously valuable to community service organizations and is likely not going to happen without the students' efforts. And, while the

Figure 7.1   Real-World Problem Statement: English Class Example

Dear Seventh-Grade Class,

Here is a real problem we face each year. Many of you come from elementary schools where there is frequent communication between your school and your parents. This helps parents feel informed about the school and involved in your work.

When you enter middle school, typically much of this communication stops. Parents feel left out and our school community suffers. The challenge for you to solve today is how to develop a system of weekly communication for your parent(s) that helps them feel informed about what we do in class, makes them feel part of the school community, and is interesting for them.

The format for this communication is up to you. Think creatively about possibilities for communication that would meet the preceding conditions. You may choose to communicate in writing, through speaking, visual images, music, or some ways I have not considered. You should generate a list of all possible ideas and then decide on the best one(s) to try, based on criteria you establish for a quality communication system you think will help connect parents to our class. You will present this communication plan to a panel of parents and school officials on Friday to get feedback on its quality before you begin its implementation.

Whatever system you choose, it must be something our class can actually do and keep up with on a weekly basis. You need to have some way to monitor the quality of this communication and to make sure it is completed each week. You also need to evaluate its effectiveness before the calendar year ends to see if it actually meets its objectives. Be sure to design a plan for this evaluation.

This is a problem for the whole class to solve, but feel free to use various groupings and strategies (including the assigning of roles) to assure this process helps build our community in a positive way. Before you begin solving this problem, I'll help set up criteria for good problem solving that should help give you direction.

Good luck! Your parents will appreciate your efforts.

Thank you,
Ms. McGillicuddy
Seventh-Grade English Teacher

need and product is very real, the stakes for the community partner and the class are relatively low as the partner won't have an immediate need for the report. The partner can choose to use the work in any way deemed appropriate.

When teachers start looking at curriculum from the perspective of "Who uses this in the real world," they can find many real-world problems to focus their students' work. Creating exhibits for a local science or historical museum, teaching material to a different age group, or addressing challenges in the community all ask students to put knowledge to use. Once teachers identify real problems to address, they can frame problem statements (see Figure 7.1) to reach the course learning objectives while serving a community need. Inevitably, this applied learning for real-world problems is engaging in a way that is hard to match through any other approach.

Community-based learning. Connect school learning to the world beyond the school walls to make it feel more real to students. Whether this connection to the community is relatively small or a deep immersion, the work of school always feels much more real when linked to the world outside school.

There is a wide continuum of community-based learning and limitless opportunities to connect school learning and the community, many of which barely require leaving the classroom. In a math class, the teacher can work with real community data—statistics from the U.S. Census or health department. A social studies teacher can study policy making at a local level, or research local history or anthropology in the lives of immigrants in the community. In English, oral histories of elderly in the area can be a source of research and writing for a study of identity and the art of biography. In science, the world surrounding the school is full of real biology, chemistry, and physics issues—investigating the health of ecosystems, air and water quality, or studying motion and force in cars or bikes.

More ambitious community-based learning might lead to a study of culture and diversity in the area, whereby each student interviews a person who was born out of the country (or out of the state at least) and researches the interviewee's country of origin. The whole class can put on a multicultural community night inviting parents, those interviewed, and the whole community to celebrate cultural diversity with food and informational posters and artifacts from around the world.

REAL AUDIENCES

Public presentations invariably raise student engagement and interest and the quality of their work. Positive peer pressure raises the stakes even for in-class presentations. The excitement and responsibility of presenting a 1940s museum or a multicultural event open to the whole community is a huge step above simply handing an assignment to the teacher.

In another school, middle school students studied the history of commerce in their area, visiting local businesses, interviewing current and retired business leaders, reading literature about the changing nature of commerce, and studying economic data. Students then created a series of skits about business in the region, using the skills of critical and creative thinking, research and analysis, and writing and speaking to reflect their developing understanding of this aspect of their community.

Some programs aim to make learning relevant by being almost completely community based. A school in Tennessee developed a semester-long ninth-grade program for sixty students working with four teachers all connected to the local NASCAR track. Students studied the math related to car design, the amount of resources used at the track, and waste produced. The physics of automotive racing offered endless lessons in science. Students did writing assignments related to their studies at the track, researched where all the supplies for the operation came from, and how far the reach was in attracting fans. Students were amazed at the wealth of jobs related to the racetrack, from marketing to food service, to maintenance, to cleaning, and to accounting. Most impressively, compared to a control group of ninth graders remaining in the "regular" program, the students in this community-based program received significantly higher grades, had fewer disciplinary problems, and improved attendance.

Community-based learning becomes service learning when the product of students' work gives back to the community. More than just community service (which has great merit in teaching students the value of good deeds and caring for others), service learning emphasizes connecting the content and skills of a class directly to addressing a community need. Conducting a study of indoor air quality for the town offices, analyzing book use at the local library, or preparing recent immigrants for their citizenship test makes academic learning useful for the community outside school.

An additional benefit of community-based learning is the unexpected discoveries and insights students may make as they dive into the complexity of real-world circumstances. Science methods that seem so straightforward in the lab might not work as smoothly out in the rain. Interviewing real people sometimes uncovers stories much more interesting than those in a textbook. Real data sometimes have outliers and disconfirming evidence that needs to be explained. This can be intriguing and exciting for students, but sometimes challenging for teachers who might be accustomed to more controlled learning situations.

PREVENTING PITFALLS: ASSURE
THE LEARNING IN SERVICE LEARNING

There are several critical elements to maximizing the learning and minimizing the uncertainty of community-based learning. Most important, teachers need to be clear about their learning objectives in planning the learning experience. Rather than start from what seems interesting in the community and then thinking about how to connect this to standards, it is usually more effective to start with course learning objectives and then to consider how this might be related to the community. Community partners are usually happy to help schools when approached with a specific request. It is much harder for most community organizations to figure out what might fit with school needs than it is to be asked to help with a specific request related to a learning goal.

Likewise, clearly identified learning objectives help set parameters for appropriate assignments and products of student work. Making expectations clear for students about what they are studying and expected to produce, just as one would with more classroom-based learning, simply changes the source and location of learning. Just as a teacher would ask students to read a chapter in a textbook and answer certain questions, the teacher can require students to gain information from the community and write a report addressing specific issues. The major difference with community-based projects is that students are much more self-motivated by work that seems more real and relevant to them than another assignment from the textbook.

Finally, students do not need to leave the building to do community-based learning. Problem statements from community organizations, even ones far removed from the local area, can articulate the real-world need and the problem to address. Through electronic communication, students can connect with the community partners and work in their own school to research and write reports and proposals to help serve the stated need.

Altering the Schedule to Provide Learning Opportunities

Anyone who has worked in schools knows there are predictable rhythms to the year. Excitement and energy in September, the long unbroken stretch through October, vacation-laden late November through January, the choppy schedule in winter, tiring demands at the end of the grading period, springtime with all sorts of reawakenings, the built up weariness of May, and the waning attention of the last days of school. The unwavering schedule of most schools exacerbates the predictability of this schedule—day 10 looks much like day 56, which is usually the same as day 127, which is probably the same as day 179 (granted, day 180 is usually a novel "fun day"). And periods 1 through 7 (or blocks 1, 2, 3, 4) every day, every year for four years of high school characterize each day. For any adolescent looking for inspiration, this unchanging schedule can become monotonous and stress laden; in fact, 71 percent of high school students report feeling often or always stressed by schoolwork (Pope, 2010).

There is nothing wrong with regularity in school scheduling. Most students greatly value structure (whether they admit this or not). But not everything worth learning happens in ninety-minute periods, and the restrictions of the schedule often override some of the most valuable educational experiences we can provide for students. Strategically varying the schedule at the right times of the year can help avoid some potentially less educational periods of school while providing learning experiences that could never happen within the confines of the bell schedule. The possibilities for "special" weeks or days are endless. Organized around clear learning goals and purposes, these can be some of the most energizing periods of the year with some of the most powerful learning for students and teachers. The following section provides ideas for special days.

Project Week. Project Week is a chance for students to practice the type of independent work they must do after graduating from school. Classes are dropped for the week as students are asked to extend their learning in self-directed, student-initiated projects under faculty supervision. These projects offer students an energizing structure for learning where they can demonstrate command of knowledge and skills from their courses throughout the year. Each student is assigned a teacher "coach" who supports and oversees the student's work. Students often choose to use Project Week for job shadowing or internships, or they develop projects that relate to course learning goals while allowing each student to pursue areas of particular interest. For example, a ninth grader may choose to demonstrate her understanding of U.S. history and environmental science and the skill of being a clear and effective communicator by developing a website detailing the debate over oil drilling in the Alaska wilderness. There are countless themes that can guide Project Week, but key to this engaging educational experience is students taking ownership for their learning, and pursuing projects meaningful to them.

Health Week. Health Week is an intensive period of time dedicated to general issues of health and wellness for individuals and the community. Organized thematically and encompassing a wide range of activities including presentations, workshops, hands-on activities, all-school events, community meals, and physical pursuits, Health Week addresses health curriculum and touches on issues central to students' lives. Health Week is a chance to bring in health professionals from the community to share their expertise from a wide range of perspectives on health and wellness. Topics to address may include nutrition, safety, first aid, mental health, consumer health, human growth and development, human sexuality, issues of substance use, diversity, environmental sustainability, and healthy living. These can all be explored on a personal, community, and global level. Health Week can thus raise awareness of a wide variety of ideas related to healthy living, and help students develop the ability to make informed, responsible, and healthy choices.

Problem-Based Community Service Week. This break in the regular schedule allows students to work in teams to use their academic skills to address real community needs. Problem statements from community partners define a particular need for which students seek a solution. A team of students, working with a teacher, determines a plan to study this problem and produce a report, solution, or service to address the community need. Like consulting teams in the workplace, students learn to work together, bringing together diverse skills and talents to work on real-world problems for a real purpose. The problem statement can frame the work to focus attention on specific learning goals while still leaving room for student creativity and ingenuity. Problem-based community service has proven a great opportunity to allow K–12 and college students to be involved in real learning for the real world, and to be of direct service to the community (see Figure 7.2).

Culture Days. These are days devoted to learning about culture and diversity. Filled with workshops, presentations, interactive exercises, shared meals, and diverse arts, the school community is enlivened by celebrating the diversity of the world around them. Culture Days offer outside

Figure 7.2   Problem-Based Service Learning Example

Dear Students,

As some of you may know, the town of Westminster, like most municipalities nationwide, incurs a high cost for solid waste disposal. This cost is likely to increase significantly in just a few years. We desperately need help in trying to lessen the costs of solid waste disposal and educating our citizens on this pressing problem.

As a representative for the Westminster selectboard, I invite you to study the solid waste management issue in our town. Specifically, we, and our voters, would benefit from a clear, professional quality presentation on the following:

- Current costs
- Projected future costs
- Ideas for alternatives to reduce our costs
- Projected savings under different scenarios
- Any insights, if possible, on how to encourage increased recycling to reduce the waste stream

The final product that would be most useful to us is a written report, complete with appropriate graphs and figures and including a one-page introductory executive summary. In addition, we invite some members of your group to present your findings at our selectboard meeting on February 12, at 7:00 at the town hall. If your findings warrant, we would appreciate having a one-page handout we could use at town meeting to begin the education process in the community.

I imagine your research to have two major pieces. One involves "number crunching" to figure out costs, what the waste stream consists of, where it goes, and where costs might be reduced. Another part determines how community members perceive recycling and how to best encourage increased recycling. This would involve some form of interviewing or surveying. I can act as a contact for this and can provide you a lot of background information.

In advance, I thank you for your help on this. We have all too little time to do the hard thinking and research needed to reach solutions for this problem. Your research will be of immense help in serving all in the Westminster community.

Sincerely,
Paul Harlow
Westminster Selectman

community members, teachers, and students the chance to share their experiences and perspectives. Through the range of "differences" students are exposed to in Culture Days, there is increased appreciation of diversity. Knowing others well is a key to respect—Culture Days can be one part of developing this kind of understanding that leads to greater valuing of the "other."

There is a balance to how much time should be in a traditional school structure and how much for these special days. As exciting as these special days can be, they take time to plan and can be so engaging that students and teachers can get consumed by the excitement. Once they have experienced the energy of these special days, students will look forward to them. At the same time, these breaks in the normal schedule can relieve some of the stress or monotony of school and make students appreciate the consistency of the regular schedule even more, making all learning more valued.

The first concern many educators express about schedule changes is "losing" time to get through the curriculum. Without belaboring the argument that our focus should be more on student learning and less on curriculum coverage, it is clear that students who are engaged with school and bring a level of interest and excitement allow time be used more effectively than needing to focus so much on managing disinterested students. A respectful school "creates" time by lessening distractions and disciplinary issues, the energy-sapping enemies of focused learning and student success. This time, in turn, can be devoted to diverse learning opportunities that tap into more wide-ranging student interests and learning styles, thus promoting a virtuous cycle of increased engagement and improved learning results.

MAKING IT REAL: SUGATA MITRA'S HOLE-IN-THE-WALL PROJECT

Michael Fullan, the preeminent researcher on school change, argues what is really needed is a fundamental change in the culture of schools. Nowhere has this idea of fundamental change in educational systems and culture been more fully explored than in the work of an Indian educator named Sugata Mitra. His Hole-in-the-Wall project is too incredible to be fully described here, but we urge you to check out his research (Inamdar & Kulkarni, 2007; Mitra et al., 2005). (See also www.hole-in-the-wall.com/Publications.html and video presentations on www .Ted.org.)

In essence, Mitra's research shows that children of all ages are capable of teaching themselves and one another, using computers and the Internet, without any adult instruction or supervision. He placed powerful computers with Internet connectivity in outdoor walls in some of the poorest villages throughout India. Cameras rolled and captured children approaching the wall, teaching themselves how to operate the touch pad, accessing the Internet, and showing other illiterate children how to do the same.

The children who used the computers spoke many different native languages, but since the Internet is in English, the children quickly taught themselves English, and subsequently began to use it in their daily interactions. Children self-organized into learning groups of between three and six, and taught and learned from each other with no adults present. This study illustrates, then, how students become highly skilled in computer literacy and usage with no adult instruction.

Mitra conducted batteries of academic tests and found that the academic gains made by children who visited the Hole-in-the-Wall computers mirrored the academic learning achieved by students in traditional schools with whom they were compared.

One of the best parts of the Hole-in-the-Wall model is perhaps the "granny cloud." Mitra added a new feature to the Hole-in-the-Wall experiments where he used cameras to "beam" two hundred grandmothers to the children while they were using the Hole-in-the-Wall computers. When the granny cloud was introduced, the academic learning of students increased even more, simply by providing—not instruction or coaching—some good old-fashioned, granny TLC!

Mitra's research on student learning, the power of emotional support, peer instruction, and self-organization challenges educators who believe that the academic environment within schools ought to focus on what teachers do, rather than on what students do. Think of the wide-ranging opportunities that are possible with an understanding that children's learning can be a self-organizing system, rather than one based on nineteenth-century factory models of industrial production.

One small example from my own, Bill's, family is noteworthy here. My son's high school requires that every student complete a senior project for graduation. The project requires each student to propose a topic; receive approval; and then, working with an adult mentor, complete the project and present the results at a spring exhibition. My son is wonderful and I love him dearly, but he is a real procrastinator when it comes to schoolwork. Like so many other high school students, he typically waits until the last minute to start a paper or do a project for school. But he has a passion for music—writing it, practicing it, performing it, and recording it.

This past summer, before beginning his senior year, he announced that he needed to clean his room—he *never* cleans his room. He meant he needed to clean *everything* out of his room, except his bed and his bureau. "Why?" we asked. "I need to start building my recording studio for my senior project," he told us. He next began researching complex digital-recording techniques. He asked if we could help him earn money to buy ProTools, a professional recording software package—"light-years ahead of GarageBand," he told us (like we knew anything about GarageBand). We saw he had picked up a stack of eight books on recording at the town library. He wasn't even supposed to start his senior project until his school approved it, but he wasn't waiting. I loved it when my son's music teacher actually called to ask him about how to use a specific tool in the GarageBand recording software that my son had been using for a few years.

Who was this kid? What had the school done with my procrastinating son? This is a great example of the power of self-organization. It also affirms what Mitra saw among the poorest children in India, and children's burning desire to learn about and do things that are meaningful and useful to them.

CONCLUSION

Thinking and learning takes energy. The energy any individual devotes to learning depends greatly on motivation, and motivation depends on individual interest. Students' motivation increases when they feel teachers care about their learning and their success. The most direct way for students to feel they matter in the classroom is to give them choices in their learning, to engage them in interesting and meaningful learning experiences, and to help them see how their learning connects to the world beyond the school walls. Above all else, we show we really care about learning for each student when we provide a wide range of learning experiences and formats—no one way works for all students; offering diverse experiences, choices, and variety in how we use time all help students feel respected as individuals and engaged in the learning process.

Finally, educators might begin their exploration of respectful teaching by doing a little "Hole-in-the-Wall" experiment of their own. Begin by thinking about the fact that smartphones students carry in their pockets may have more computing power than the entire computer network within a typical school. Why not begin working with students to figure out ways to use these tools instructionally, rather than fearing them or spending energy trying to restrict them? This exercise may open up the school, teachers, and students to the world in new and exciting ways. Wouldn't that get everyone's attention and show how respectful teachers and school leaders work with students in the school?

SIMPLE SUMMARY: STAGE FOUR SPECIFICS

- Determine what you, your colleagues, and students mean by respectful teaching and student engagement.
- Provide more choices and options for students.
- Apply learning to solve real problems because this makes learning deeper, more meaningful, and relevant.
- Use the community and extend learning beyond the walls of the school.
- Require students to present their learning to real audiences besides just the teacher.
- Alter your school schedule to provide different time frames for learning, applying knowledge, and presenting what has been learned.
- Provide students with access to technology, and allow self-organized learning to occur. Prepare to be amazed at what students will and can do.

BOOK STUDY QUESTIONS

1. From a student's perspective what are the "most respectful" and "most effective" teaching practices, activities, and programs your school currently offers? How do these differ from other experiences in the school?

2. What are some ideas you have for more classroom-level and school-wide attention to improve relationships, develop more engaged learners, or to personalize learning?

3. How can you increase choice for students in their learning (while still focusing on targeted learning results)?

4. What opportunities are there in your classes to connect to "the real world" and make learning more authentic?

5. Does Mitra's work on self-organized learning have relevance to our schools? How might you enable students to organize themselves to pursue learning on their own terms?

6. How do technology and self-organization affect student engagement, motivation, peer respect, and sense of belonging?

8

Stage Five: Moving Forward Together

Sustainability and Continuous Improvement

The heart and mind work as one in our students and ourselves.

Parker Palmer, *The Courage to Teach* (2007, p. 64)

ON TO YEAR TWO: AN ADULT LEADERSHIP TEAM MEMBER REFLECTS ON THE JOURNEY

It seems like forever since we formed our student leadership team at Westfield High School, recruiting a ragtag mix of kids who, I worried, would not take any of this seriously. Then we did our school climate survey and things started to roll.

It was easy to agree on goals, and the action projects just flowed from there. It was really a small step to get teachers to agree that our teacher-selected student of the month program could be improved and expanded. We could turn it into a monthly celebration of many more students, teachers, and staff for all the great things they are doing to make this school a better place. We have also gotten pretty good at routinely sharing the many nominations for these "official" awards and good deeds as part of our data wall, which shows everybody the work we are trying to do to improve this school. These fairly simple projects gave our leadership team a sense of immediate success, and helped give us the confidence and energy for the more ambitious effort to try out "Periods of Discovery" the last few days of the year.

The feedback we have received from some teachers, and lots of students, is that they are excited about our work. We believe that we are beginning to make some important changes in our school. Teachers and students feel they are working together toward common ends, and our school's whole approach to solving problems is changing from just reacting to problems to organizing new approaches with students and teachers working together. We have a lot to build on—the student and teacher leadership teams are working well, we are becoming more visible in the school, and we all feel a sense of accomplishment from our successes so far.

The trajectory is definitely up, but we are a long way from being a truly strong school—there is still too much student apathy, too many lifeless classes, too much plodding through a static curriculum—but we have a foothold now and we need to make sure this work continues and grows next year.

This next year is going to be crucial. If we can build on the excitement of our student team and the structures we already have in place, extend our reach to gain more support by students and teachers, and work to have an impact on more classrooms and existing programs to improve the way we all treat one another, then we'll be able to make a real difference in this school.

CHANGE IS A PROCESS, NOT AN EVENT

Stages One through Four define year one of the SafeMeasures™ process, the beginning of climate change, not the end. Stage Five, and beyond, is about continuity in subsequent years. Instead of new initiatives and new programs each year creating reform fatigue, the SafeMeasures process is an ongoing, overarching strategy for problem solving on any issue, capacity building, and climate improvement that will create the conditions for more effective learning for all.

For a school to sustain the work begun through the first four stages of this process, it is imperative that schools build on the foundations of year one to *enhance* action projects, *extend* engagement to new supporters and into new areas, and *empower* teachers and students to help shape the school culture. All of this functions to help every child and every teacher succeed.

We all wish the change process was easier—come up with a good project, implement, and *voila*, all our problems in schools go away. Unfortunately, that is not typically the way things work.

We've all heard the adage that "change is a process, not an event." Even the best projects we've seen only work for some of the people some of the time. As discussed in Chapter 6, there simply is no one right way that will solve even a well-defined problem. And, most issues in schools are so intertwined that one issue can't be "fixed" without confronting a bunch of others. For example, something as simple as trying to improve test scores by serving breakfast on testing day requires finding the resources to pay for the food, getting teachers to take on extra responsibilities notifying students and families, supervising the cafeteria, adjusting for some students' food allergies, dealing with parent complaints about intruding into family dietary choices, and getting the custodians to clean up the cafeteria another time during their already busy day. One can then imagine the list of steps involved in getting an entire school to change.

Changing school climate is less about any single project or result than about establishing a pervasive schoolwide commitment to the success of every child, and making every individual in the school feel valued and part of the school's success. This feeling comes partly through concrete activities such as celebrating student accomplishments or displaying high-quality student work. More important are the processes that give each individual in the school community the sense that they matter and make a difference in helping to shape their own school experience and the experiences of each person with whom they interact at school.

One-time actions, such as asking a few students to serve on a committee or a year-end chance for students to give feedback on their school experience, have limited impact on a school. On the other hand, students' and teachers' ongoing and systemic involvement creates a deeper feeling of empowerment to make positive change in their schools. For change to become systemic, no single program or practice is sufficient. Multiple structures—such as student council, students serving on hiring committees, a student-led judiciary, monthly check-in meetings between students and the principal, advisories, annual school surveys and evaluations, and an ongoing student leadership team—establish a culture of student involvement in school improvement.

Likewise, multiple projects and activities—such as honoring a wide range of students of the week, posting a greater variety of accomplishments in trophy cases, portfolio assessments and report cards that acknowledge more wide ranging intelligences, more choice within classes, schedule changes such as Project Week, and time in school for students to share diverse talents—can build appreciation for the unique qualities of each individual and increase respect schoolwide. We must find ways to engage not the most innovative risk takers as supporters of these programs and practices; we need to gain widespread teacher support and the school leaders' commitment to maintain these initiatives as priorities.

KEY ELEMENTS OF SUSTAINABLE CHANGE

While process is important, what ultimately count are results. That is why we try hard to clearly connect the *means* (improving relationships, school climate, student engagement, teacher and effectiveness) with the *ends* (decreasing discipline problems, and improving and deepening student learning). Simply pushing to stop bullying or for higher test scores alone won't work to achieve sustained school improvement and reform. In his highly respected review of research on school reform, *The New Meaning of Educational Change*, Michael Fullan (2001) identifies eight key elements of successful change (p. 44) for school leaders to keep in mind as they work to bring about and sustain effective school improvement of any kind:

1. Define *closing the gap* (from where you are to where you want to be) as the overarching goal.

2. Tap into people's dignity and sense of respect.

3. Ensure that the best (or the right) people are working on the problem.

4. Recognize that all successful strategies are socially based and action oriented. We accomplish change by building relationships and by "doing" rather than by elaborate planning.

5. Assume lack of capacity is the initial problem and then work on it continuously.

6. Stay the course through continuity of direction by leveraging leadership.

7. Establish conditions for the evolution of positive pressure.

8. Use these strategies to build public confidence.

This list, Fullan emphasizes, is not a menu from which to pick and choose; schools need them all for a "well-balanced reform agenda" (p. 44).

Stage Five of the SafeMeasures process, sustainability and continuous improvement, asks school leaders to understand and incorporate Fullan's principles of successful, sustainable school change to ensure that the process lasts and is effective over time. Next we expand on the first four of these principles that are most closely related to Stage Five.

Closing the Gaps

By the time a school gets to Stage Five, both student and adult leaders must be clear on what they are working to achieve. There are two important "gaps" that SafeMeasures helps schools to understand and address. First is the gap between learning and behavioral outcomes for different groups of students in any school. We show schools how to use school climate and achievement data to better appreciate, understand, and address the different needs of different clusters of students. We use a response to intervention (RTI) model to show schools how their students fall into at least three distinct tiers related to both academic and behavioral outcomes. This tiered framework helps schools see how different strategies for change are required for students at each tier, whether academically or behaviorally.

The second gap we help student leaders and adults address is the divergence in school climate perceptions that students and teachers report on climate surveys. Exposing this adult-student perception gap does a great deal to motivate teachers in trying to better understand what is really happening with school climate. By working more closely with their students, teachers can learn a lot about what students see and experience, and thereby better develop effective strategies to improve climate and learning.

Dignity and Respect

SafeMeasures is a process of participatory school inquiry, not a generic prescription for school change. SafeMeasures is a locally driven, cyclical process of data collection and analysis, goal setting, action steps, and reassessment. To initiate the process, adult leaders and teachers invite diverse student experts on school climate issues to serve as their partners in school reform and improvement. What could be more respectful? With student, teacher, and parent data guiding consensus about a school's greatest needs, local student and teacher leadership teams, not some outside expert, establish goals for school improvement. The embedded knowledge within a school of its unique culture, history, and traditions inform the specific benchmarks, and realistic expectations for change are set to help the system move forward. We believe, as was stated by Sarah Lawrence-Lightfoot (2000) in her book *Respect: An Exploration*, that "respect is a verb" (p. 57)—it is something we do, not just discuss. We hope that SafeMeasures is a process, then, that "does respect."

The Best People Working on the Problem

The best people to work on the problem, once again, are those who know best the challenges and opportunities within the school. Diverse groups of students and teachers bring knowledge to the table essential to understanding the true nature of bullying, discipline, dropouts, or disengaged learners. They can also be invaluable sources of new ideas for addressing these problems that may never occur to adults working in isolation. No matter how "expert" these adults may believe they are, those who know a school best, from direct experience day in and day out, are students.

Socially Based and Action-Oriented Change

The SafeMeasures process is all about building relationships and "doing change." The diverse group of student leaders comes together and forms bonds through initial team building exercises. While these first activities are valuable, team members really bond when they take on the roles of leaders for collective action. Becoming a school climate researcher, speaking to the faculty about differences in teacher-student perceptions, presenting results to a school board, and leading school projects with peers bring students and teachers together to plan and implement projects and activities. The collaborative work of improving a school for everyone changes school climate and culture. As Fullan (2001) notes, all successful change has an "action bias." The whole SafeMeasures process is aimed toward Stage Four: Action Planning and Implementation. Including students and teachers in the change process builds ownership and enthusiasm that moves action forward.

Reacting to problems one at a time is the death knell of schools. SafeMeasures avoids this and is dedicated to developing organizational capacity—learning how to bring the real experts to the table, collect data from stakeholders, analyze information and set goals, take action, and then adjust to better reach the goals. This process can be applied to any school challenge, establishing practices that solve problems while reshaping school climate and culture. With a common sense of purpose, administrators, teachers, and students are involved at each stage of the process. They work together to create positive energy, leverage the human resources within the school, and build public confidence that all voices are heard and the "system" is working in harmony for the greater good.

ENHANCE, EXTEND, AND EMPOWER

It can be useful to think of sustainability of reform through three related frames. The first perspective is how to *enhance* initial efforts. Based on formative feedback, how can action projects be improved to be more effective? This is a basic step in being better at whatever a school is doing. If a school has been trying out morning meetings, how can this be more engaging for all students, more diverse in its goals, more smooth in its flow? If a school held Culture Day last year, how can it be done even better this year? Should it be expanded to multiple days? Can students lead some of the workshops this year in addition to adult presenters?

Next, and more critical for maintaining and building momentum, is looking at how to *extend* action projects. This can happen on several levels:

- *Involve and affect more people.* An action project may start as a pilot with one grade or a few classrooms or teachers. If the project looks promising, it can be expanded to include all grades or teachers. Likewise, an activity can become more frequent—so a monthly all-school meeting may become weekly, a one time Period of Discovery can become a monthly event.
- *Infiltrate more parts of the school system.* Schools are complex places. Ideally, school climate is consistently strong throughout the system. So a project that starts in one part of the system, such as celebrating diversity in honoring student of the month, may be extended to celebrate the value of individuals throughout the system (teacher of the month, community contributor of the month, honoring staff members

regularly, sharing positive stories of students' and adults' accomplishments during school board meetings, highlighting individuals in the school and on the school website, etc.). A small project to honor more students may lead to a culture of bringing out the best in everybody by celebrating the positive throughout the system.

- *Add more ambitious projects.* While it makes sense to start small, some of the best, most comprehensive projects are bigger in scope and impact. Project Week—with what the Coalition of Essential Schools labels as "students as workers, teachers as coach"—can be one of the most powerful strategies for helping students shine as they pursue personal passions, demonstrate self-direction, and deepen relationships. Once teachers and students experience the potent results and positive energy of a Project Week, there may be interest in adding another similar week at some other time in the year, perhaps focused on a particular learning area such as science or the arts or cultural diversity. In some schools, jumping right into Project Week can seem too big a leap, so a smaller effort can lead to more ambitious actions later. For instance, a reasonable starting point could be to offer greater choice in products or topics within some classes or provide an option for twelfth graders to pursue independent senior projects.

- *Attack a different level of the Respect Continuum.* Many schools start their climate work trying to move beyond compliance through developing better relationships between students and teachers. This can create a more friendly tone to life in the hallways, but a next step may be to improve respect by looking at what occurs in the classroom for learners. Although students and teachers may get along between classes, this has limited impact if classes feel dull, meaningless, and unmotivating. Extending initial efforts to build relationships by creating more engaging and personalized learning experiences for students can be real "rocket fuel" for improving school climate, and academic results.

- *Work on another goal or standard.* Happily, some projects achieve results where the targeted goal is met. This can lead to looking at other issues and goals worth addressing. Maybe initially action projects were designed to assure each child had a trusted adult in the school for support through advisories, individualized projects, and outside-of-school events such as an all class hike where kids interacted with adults in different roles. Formative and summative assessment may show that now 100 percent of the students say they have an adult in school they can turn to for support. This is a great achievement, but it doesn't solve all challenges in school climate. It may now be time to find ways to empower more students through school council and judiciary and student representation on the board and hiring committees. Or, students and teachers might be ready to work together to revise the school discipline system. The goal is to build on successes, but also extend to the logical next issue to work to continuously improve school climate and learning.

In many ways, these extensions sustain energy for school climate and learning. One successful project can lead to another, and positive results generate momentum for undertaking other projects. Especially when projects expand involvement, invite more participants, and enlist greater support, the capacity evolves for future projects using these now engaged individuals.

Sustainability ultimately depends on time, energy, personnel, and capacity. The adult resources in schools are finite. There are only so many staff and each of them has many demands on their time. Students, however, can be a vast untapped resource; they outnumber adults in any school by a large factor. The third frame for sustaining reform over time, then, is to *empower* students to help lead efforts for a positive school climate. Students help in planning by knowing what is likely to work effectively and are a source of the person power needed to implement action projects. Perhaps more significant, as students feel greater respect in school—having better relationships with each other and with teachers, being more engaged in learning, and feeling empowered as valued members of the school community—the many distractions of less respectful schools decrease. Less time and energy needs to be devoted to disciplinary issues. Students and teachers are subsequently able to focus more on teaching and learning.

Structures developed in the school change process can become institutionalized to ensure sustainability. Ongoing meetings for the student-teacher leadership team, monthly check-ins for the student leaders and principal, a well defined policy-making function for student council, a student judiciary or peer mediation group, annual surveys on school climate, rituals to celebrate each individual in the school, and other structures can come to define and support the school culture.

MAKE A MULTIYEAR COMMITMENT

The SafeMeasures process in Stages One through Four really focused on year one, when the school commits to the school improvement process, creates leadership teams, gathers data and sets goals, and begins action planning and implementation. This first year is crucial for establishing the no-fault culture that looks honestly at challenges while acknowledging the hard work and goodwill of every individual in school. Serving as the foundation for shared efforts to improve the school, this is no small accomplishment. Unless administrators, teachers, and students feel safe in the process, there is no way any real work can be accomplished.

This cultural shift immediately impacts the development of a more constructive and respectful school climate. There is a growing sense that "we are all in this together" and a resulting feeling of efficacy. Relationships developed through meaningful work together and focusing on the positives build energy for further change.

This all takes time, and even with the most efficient process, it usually isn't until spring that the action planning gets off the ground. As stated earlier, it takes much more than one great action project to make a real difference. The first-year projects are a starting point—they raise visibility, generate momentum, and hopefully begin to address some goals. But these are just a start.

Year two is a chance to enhance the effectiveness of the now more experienced leadership teams and build on the previous year's projects. New leadership team members can provide the capacity and energy for extending projects to impact the school more widely. As relationships grow stronger, attention can move to making more connections between school climate and academic learning. Efforts can begin to move up the Respect Continuum, creating more engaged and personalized learning, and finding ways to empower students and teachers to contribute more fully to improvement efforts.

The second year can crystallize the culture and climate of the school—institutionalizing practices that reflect commitments to creating a respectful school that works for every child. Undoubtedly, the many challenges in school are not going to be eradicated by a strong leadership process and even a good number of action projects. Each group of students brings new needs and the dynamic global world brings new demands on schools.

Year three (and beyond) is the time to use all the strong processes and structures established through SafeMeasures to do the steady and rewarding work of continuous improvement. This is the model of all successful organizations, whether in the world of business or education: build solid processes, use tools to measure progress, make adjustments, and continuously work to make things better and more effective.

FORMATIVE ASSESSMENT: A CRITICAL PART OF THE PROCESS

Wishing we could design action projects that worked perfectly impedes the process of real change. In seeking the "perfect" design, we can be led to plan almost endlessly, only to be disappointed when our tremendous efforts fall short of the goal (thereby creating a rational aversion to subsequent efforts for further reform).

A more useful model for change involves trying out a few projects with a well-defined goal; piloting the effort on a trial basis, maybe with only a small group of students or teachers; and then using formative assessment—check-ins and data gathering as the projects proceed—to see how things are going and how the project can be modified to increase impact. Not only does this result in more effective projects with reduced pressure on everyone to get everything "right," but the shared effort generates goodwill. Everyone aims to do what's best for all, work together, and commit to continuous school improvement. This transforms school climate and thereby changes the school culture.

Formative assessment can be formal or informal. The main questions are as follows:

- What is working well?
- What are the results and for whom?
- What needs to be modified?
- What are the logical next steps?

Ideally, these questions are answered through a rigorous, scientific study. One solid approach to formative and summative assessment is to readminister the full SafeMeasures survey. The results will help identify indicators of improved climate. The school can then verify these through focus groups and interviews to elucidate how a particular action project is creating the observed results.

Given the finite time and resources in schools, it may be more realistic, and still quite useful, to employ "quick dipstick" assessments to check on how things are going and what should be modified. This formative feedback may involve reflective discussions with the project implementation team or student leadership team, a focus group with a selected group of students and/or teachers, a quick survey of a randomly or purposefully selected group of students (maybe using a few intentionally selected questions from the SafeMeasures survey), or even a check-in with advisory or homeroom groups to collect more broad reflections.

Unlike summative assessment that aims to generate reliable and valid data on impact, formative assessment is really about useful feedback that can help make adjustments to improve results. Interesting research from high-tech startups demonstrates that most successful firms "go live" very early with more simplistic versions of their new technology and then modify continuously in response to customer feedback. Being open to making changes "on the fly" not only can improve project effectiveness but also reinforces the message that students and teachers are working together with genuine commitment to the best results for all.

ALIGNING SCHOOL CLIMATE AND LEARNING: DEMONSTRATE A BALANCED APPROACH

As we've explained throughout this book, school climate is more a means to an end than an end in itself. The central purpose for schools remains focused on student learning in general and academic learning in particular. While school climate is instrumental to all other learning results, it can seem "touchy-feely" when it is a goal in itself. While we certainly value a pleasant school climate, if this doesn't impact learning results, efforts will generate limited support over time.

While initial climate work might be less focused on academic results, to sustain momentum over time, the links between school climate and learning need to be made clear for both students and adults. Students are savvy. If they see respect and positive relationships touted in school assemblies and on posters in the halls, but feel powerless in the face of their teachers' absolute authority in the classroom every day, then they feel manipulated and quickly become jaded. It is essential that school climate work moves from behavioral topics such as bullying and school violence into the day-to-day reality of classrooms, where students spend the vast majority of their time. Moving from discussions about compliance with rules and friendly relations to respectful teaching and learning makes the issue of respect more authentic to students.

Teachers know they are ultimately responsible for the learning results of their students. Climate efforts that take time away from academic learning run counter to this focus. Ultimately, climate may be most effectively addressed in the classroom, with attention to more engaged and personalized learning experiences.

Engaged learning may involve the greatest shift in power relations of the whole change process. It means overcoming the "two great sins" in teaching (Wiggins & McTighe, 2005)—using "fun" activities that have little educational purpose (more common in elementary schools) and "covering" content even if no one pays any attention (seen more often in high schools). In either case, misplaced emphasis on fun or coverage overrides the more purposeful focus on results—what students actually know, understand, and can do as a result of a learning experience. The shift in power must move from what the teacher is doing to what the students are doing. Instead of "I taught it," we need to assure that kids learned it.

This doesn't mean we just let students do whatever they want or study only what they find interesting. Rather, engaged and personalized learning takes thoughtful planning, using what we know about how the brain works and what is motivating for students, to create learning experiences that actively connect students to the curriculum. A high school religions course I, Rick, taught raised the big questions every teen seems to ask: What is the purpose of life? What does it mean to live a good life? Is there a moral code that can guide us? How do you deal with challenges, celebrations, life, and death? This course involved extensive writing and reading and higher order thinking (as well as connecting to history, sociology, geography, and political science). This kind of meaningful learning pushes kids to do some of their best work, while developing self-awareness and understanding that will serve them well beyond their time in school.

One more power shift for sustained change is alleviating the stranglehold the schedule imposes on learning. Not all learning occurs in ninety- (or forty-five) minute chunks (or in classrooms with twenty to thirty kids). When we think of life beyond school, we can see the need to help students develop the capacity for more independent work that takes self-responsibility to design and complete. Life skills also develop through more extended projects that take time management and organization, more collaborative work that builds skills in working with others in a diverse global world, and more complex problem solving that requires flexibility and decision making needed for a rapidly changing world (Wagner, 2008). These kinds of learning experiences can't always fit into ninety-minute periods—organizing some special days or weeks for students to do more extended project-based work, more community-based learning, and more complex explorations is essential to developing the kinds of diverse learning experiences. These are the experiences that can provide all students the opportunities to work within their comfort zone as well as challenge them to stretch their boundaries.

Moving the focus to desired learning results for students, and the conditions that support these, is what aligns climate work with academic learning goals. We know adults can only push students so far to improve their academic performance—only when each student develops the desire to do well, feels connected to school, and sees himself or herself as a valued member of the community will the motivation exist to perform at a high level. This occurs through the creation of respectful schools and respectful classrooms.

GUIDEPOSTS FOR SUSTAINABILITY

Sustain leadership teams. Adult leaders on the design team may change from year to year. Keeping an active, engaged, well-trained adult design team in place is very important. Maintaining administrative support from year to year is also critical, especially when there is administrative turnover. Steps must be taken to gain the support and engagement of a new principal or superintendent.

Student leadership has the inherent problem that students continually get older and graduate from our schools. Leadership capacity developed in the course of reform work can be lost as students or teachers move on from the school. Schools that successfully sustain their leadership teams continue to add new students who truly represent the diversity in the student body—including differences in ethnicity, learning style, level of accomplishment in school, and even cliques. Each year, a leadership team may require adult support to reassemble as a team, to form a clear team identity, to build social and personal bonds among team members, to continue to publicize the team name and mission, and to continually share the results of its work with peers and adults.

Communicate goals, efforts, and results using data walls. To keep attention on school climate initiatives, it helps to keep the goals and results visible. Many schools create "data walls" to publicize efforts and progress toward identified goals. Data walls are powerful tools in the change process—raising awareness, building interest, showing what is being attempted, and demonstrating results. Data walls can be used to post a variety of information. An early iteration may include SafeMeasures data along with goals identified by the leadership team.

As action projects are developed, they can be publicized on the data wall, along with information that can enlist participation with these projects from students and adults. Data walls can celebrate student and teacher work that results from action projects—interesting class assignments, student created products, and drafts of committee documents to improve school policies can also be posted. Data walls make a great space for sharing student voice and action.

Most important, data walls can highlight accomplishments and communicate results. Graphs can chart response to interventions. Student or teacher quotes from interviews can share exciting or emotional thoughts. Numbers can reflect participation rates, statistical findings, and changes in survey data. These data keep all "eyes on the prize"—holding all in the school community accountable for the goals and results of efforts for school improvement.

Develop infrastructure, policies, and roles. It quickly becomes apparent how students and teachers can be powerful resources for school leadership. Once this is recognized, it can take a shift in thinking to consider how to include them in more aspects of school improvement. The list of places where teachers and students can contribute to the business of school leadership is almost endless—curriculum review and development, policy making, program design, evaluation processes, professional development efforts, goal setting, hiring committees, and on and on. With new roles, it can be necessary to develop new policies that are more open to greater involvement of students, teachers, and community members. While respecting confidentiality and other legal imperatives, there may be other changes that need to be made to allow students and teachers to serve in official positions (such as being a member of the school board or executive council), to be in the building for work outside the school day, or to travel for leadership-related work.

Solving real problems with students is a very powerful learning opportunity for students and adults as well. Developing a school culture that embraces student and teacher empowerment, and including all stakeholders in helping to improve the school, are important keys to sustaining school change.

Preserve data and work. Another power shift for enlisting greater participation in school improvement is making information accessible to those who need it. Computer technologies allow storage of a wide range of materials, from data to documents to video and audio productions. Using password protected V-books (virtual books), wikis, or open source websites, schools can help teams update and store their work.

This shared storage serves several functions: (1) documenting progress and making information available over time, (2) serving as a historical record that reflects changes over time, (3) celebrating accomplishments, and (4) facilitating ongoing work that is passed from one school year to the next. Obviously, not all problems in school can be "fixed" following the school calendar.

Reflect on and celebrate successes. It is essential to celebrate successes—often. Another old adage tells us we catch more flies with honey. A big part of developing a positive school climate is to celebrate the positive—assume the best in everyone, look for strengths, acknowledge small steps forward, and reward accomplishments. In even the most difficult schools, there are countless acts of kindness, hard work, and real growth every day. Positive energy creates more positive energy. Reflecting on successes offers an opportunity for each individual to make personal connections with what works. Celebrations can also be a form of modeling. They can allow everyone to put themselves in the shoes of those whose work is being honored and to do some soul searching about what they could do to make meaningful contributions.

Create a culture of celebration. Incorporate different ways to honor success as part of the school culture: send out press releases; post items at the school entry; e-mail a monthly newsletter, not only to parents but to any community members who might be interested; write stories on the school website; post student work in halls and in the district office and maybe in local businesses; have students create museums of their work and public performances that show off their accomplishments (and bring these to the public at the town hall, mall, or elderly center); and let students and teachers commend individuals at all school meetings.

Avoid making awards a special occasion for an elite group. We want every child to feel special, not just a select few—find venues to recognize all the positive things, both small and large, that happen daily to make schools function as well as they do. Use post-test data to show evidence of successful change. Use survey results to show measurable progress. Comparing changes on individual indicators over time is affirming and can help recalibrate goals and benchmarks. Qualitative data (and anecdotal stories) can complement quantitative data to offer a rich picture of the results.

Use media and community involvement. The public wants their schools to succeed. Everyone knows the importance of investing in our children and our future. As citizens, we all want to know our taxes are being used effectively. But, the public tends to know very little about what goes on in schools beyond what they hear in the press and on the streets. And, the press has a bias (and duty) to publish news of problems when they occur. Schools can do a much better job improving the flow of information to the media and the larger public. Local papers are often hungry for school-related stories and larger regional papers often look for "feel good" stories for their Sunday editions. Identifying a few teachers, parents, and students to become school "reporters" is a great job for those who want to be involved in showing what works in the school.

Schools can send press releases about all the great things going on in school—interesting class projects, new educational programs, student performances, and extracurricular activities beyond sports. Invite the public to everything and use mass e-mail with lists from the chamber of commerce, rotary, and other community leaders to "show off" school events. Make schoolwork more transparent by having teachers post curriculum, assignments, and student work on the school website.

Be strategic in using "social influencers" to lead public perceptions. Figure out key individuals in the community who shape public opinion and cultivate them as school supporters. Invite these people to serve on graduation portfolio or senior project evaluation committees, or to serve as judges at a student film festival or some other academically focused student presentation. Use these folks as an advisory council for the student and faculty leadership teams. Ask these influencers to serve as mentors for students or partners for teachers in developing extended learning experiences. Most people are honored to be asked to help and value being given a clear role to help support their local schools.

MAKING IT REAL: TALKING WALLS

Data walls are used in schools to publicly share information—promoting school goals, displaying data, and sharing student and teacher work. The students and teachers at Andover Elementary Middle School (AEMS) took this concept in a whole new direction. In the second year of their work on school climate with us, they learned about the concept of a "talking wall" and immediately wanted to create one in their school. Instead of using the wall as we usually do to report on projects related to school climate, they took a more artful approach.

We told them about Margy Burns-Knight who wrote two wonderful books called *Talking Walls* (1992) and *Talking Walls: The Story Continues* (1997). The fourth- to eighth-grade students were fascinated by the idea of a wall that talked. They contacted Margy and also Anne Sibley-O'Brien, the artist who created the marvelous paintings that became the illustrations for both books. The adult leadership team wrote an artist-in-residency grant to secure funding to bring Margy and Anne to Andover.

Margy and the teachers developed and taught lessons on world geography and cultural diversity, noting similarities and differences among peoples throughout the world using talking walls. The books' illustrations showed different walls such as the Vietnam Memorial in Washington, Hadrian's Wall in England, the Wailing Wall in Jerusalem, and the Prayer Wheel Walls in Tibet. Each wall tells an important story about the ways that people come together as a community.

Through these lessons, the Andover students came to better understand the concept of community and what makes each unique. This led to schoolwide discussions about respecting differences; how each individual has a distinctive set of talents and interests that makes them who they are; and how all of their differences, similarities, abilities, and interests make up their school community.

Anne Sibley O'Brien came to the school as a visiting artist. She worked with the student leadership team and their teacher mentors to plan for a talking wall of their own. The student leaders and Anne explained to each class that every child in the school would create a portrait of himself or herself showing things that made him or her unique.

Once the individual sketches were complete, each class went to the gymnasium and used the assembled scaffold and ladders to create individual portraits on the talking wall. Each student had an assigned space mapped out across fifty feet of the wall. The teachers made a frame out of handprints surrounding all the portraits of the students, signifying the support that they gave to every student in this community. The wall was striking. It captured the spirit of this learning community so vividly that the wall has become an icon for AEMS.

For over ten years, teachers at AEMS have used their talking wall as the focus for discussions on community, and as the symbol of school unity and caring for one another. A parent volunteer expertly photographed the AEMS talking wall and made beautiful postcards that are used for every form of communication between the school, parents, and the community.

Talking walls in many schools—adorned with data, action steps, and results of student leadership efforts—work well as tools for communicating student action, empowerment, and school improvement. They fit with the current preoccupation with results, data, and evidence of change. Andover's talking wall represents a collective act of community, an action step that helped shape and strengthen their community. For years now, the AEMS wall has symbolized the connections between teachers and students, the unique nature of every student in that school, and a celebration, in bright colors and sheer size, of the vibrancy of their school community—one that values youth voice, engagement, empowerment, and creativity as its core values.

Source: Jane Slayton, Principal, Andover Elementary Middle School, Andover, NH. Inspired by the work of Margy Burns Knight and Annie Sibley O'Brian.

CONCLUSION

In Stage Five, school leaders, both students and adults, develop new skills and knowledge about leadership and change. They begin to more fully understand that change is an ongoing process. It requires the development of a set of positive relationships within the school. It is a process of ongoing action and assessment. It requires time for personal and professional reflection and self-improvement—free of judgment and condemnation, but not devoid of personal responsibility for the success of our students and colleagues.

As Michael Fullan's research emphasizes, sustainable school change involves diverse stakeholders, is action oriented, focuses on building capacity, and leverages the leadership and expertise of the right people to ensure continuity and impact. Creating inclusive leadership teams, collecting data, setting goals, and implementing action plans is a superb starting point. These steps create the conditions upon which school climate and culture can grow and set the stage for sustaining these changes over the long-term.

Stage Five is when student leadership teams and teachers extend and expand upon their initial efforts, broaden their work into new areas, incorporate new supporters, and empower new stakeholders in shared work. These efforts allow us to create the schools that we envision will be needed if each of our students is to be successful and respectful of others as they go through their lives in the next decade of the twenty-first century.

SIMPLE SUMMARY: STAGE FIVE

- Develop a well-balanced, long-term school reform agenda by focusing on the key elements of successful change as discussed by Fullan.
- Work to extend, enhance, and empower as a means of growing support for and expanding participation in change efforts within your school.
- Make a strategic, multiyear commitment to linking initiatives whose purposes are to improve school climate and learning.
- Use formative assessment data to document and publicize your school's progress toward achieving school climate goals.
- Continually emphasize personalization, engagement, and empowerment of students and teachers as the chief means of improving school climate and learning.
- Anticipate the many challenges of sustaining your efforts—such as turnover in teaching staff and administration and graduation of student leaders.
- Incorporate new priorities into your school climate work as the school, and the world around it, changes and evolves.
- Showcase and celebrate evidence of continuous improvement and success.

BOOK STUDY QUESTIONS

1. In what ways was the AEMS talking wall an act of community?

2. What current school improvement efforts at your school are most important to you and worth keeping? How can they be enhanced?

3. What are the logical extensions to what you are doing currently? Are there new actions to undertake that would supplement current efforts?

4. What level(s) should enhancements take in your setting? What can be done to involve more people, reach further into school systems, initiate more ambitious projects, move up the Respect Continuum, and address new goals?

5. What does empowerment look like in your school? What impedes empowerment of students? How could your school institutionalize structures that support youth voice, choice, and empowerment that would support student engagement and learning?

9

The Road Ahead

Transforming School Climate and Learning

Call up in imagination the ordinary school-room, its time schedules, schemes of classification, of examination and promotion, of rules of order . . . If then you contrast this scene with what goes on in the family, for example, you will appreciate what is meant by the school being a kind of institution sharply marked off from any other form of social organization.

John Dewey, *Experience and Education* (1938/1998, p. 18)

WHEN WILL THE TIME BE RIGHT?

Albert Einstein once said that insanity is "doing the same thing over and over again and expecting different results." Schools continue to do the same things year in and year out, decade after decade, even if their results are inadequate, despite the fact that our society's needs are changing every day.

Today, many students, parents, and teachers challenge the wisdom and effectiveness of what our schools are doing. Yet it is still difficult to get people to listen and to act on new educational ideas.

CONTINUED RESISTANCE, GROWING HOPE

How it is that schools have so fiercely resisted modernization, personalization, and fundamental readjustments over the past century? We believe that students can help the adults in their schools finally begin to address the limitations of these old systems and beliefs. Collaborative change processes like SafeMeasures™, that seek to engage and empower students, helping them to exercise their voice and participate as partners in school reform, offer students and their schools hope that we can do better. When students from all sectors within a school share their experiences and stories as learners about those respectful teachers and respectful classrooms that really work for them, then we begin to see the possibilities for change. When diverse student leaders communicate their passionate concerns about the problems and injustices they see inside their schools every day, adults pay closer attention to the need for change. When students share their fresh, commonsense ideas for making schools more responsive to their and their peers' personal, social, and learning needs, it provides a powerful antidote to the factory model of schooling that has persisted since early in the last century.

We have seen how students' voices and ideas "soften up" even the hardest, most intractable, entrenched, and resistant teachers and help them recall the reasons they wanted to become teachers in the first place. Just as my, Bill's, student Samantha Smith and her peers gave voice to the absurdity of the impending nuclear holocaust during the height of the cold war, so too can students today show us the absurdity of many of our current educational practices, systems, and problems. These voices make us want to do better and give us hope for the future. These young people are eager to be engaged in learning, to solve real problems, and to hear the answer to their most asked question, "*Why* do we have to learn this?"

There are many wonderful examples of successful schools, systems, and models that educational leaders can look to, learn from, and apply to their own communities. These will help lead us forward and create schools that live up to the expectations of our students. From the Compass School and Met Schools in New England to High Tech High in California, there are schools serving diverse student populations in a personalized, responsive, and respectful manner that shows powerful results. Unfortunately, many of these model, respect-filled schools operate at the margin of the public school system. Collaborative action research, with students actively involved in the change process, can serve as a vehicle within any school to impact school climate and learning.

Our work has shown that by using student-led, collaborative action research, school leaders can overcome resistance to change. Educators can gain a clearer perspective about the realities of school life occurring around them every day. We have seen collaborative action research bring even the most jaded educators to the table; we see how the process helps them take a fresh look at the kind of educator they want to be, and the kind of school community they want to help create.

SCHOOL CLIMATE AS A COHERENT FRAMEWORK FOR UNDERSTANDING SCHOOLS

The importance of school climate and its powerful effects on schools and learning has never been better understood. Recent research by neurologists and those interested in how the human brain learns best clearly shows the negative impact that stress, threats, and negative emotions can have on learning (Jensen, 2008b). Since the school shootings at Columbine and those in other schools, every school leader now understands how students who are marginalized, humiliated, or socially isolated by their peers can explode into violence and inflict painful revenge on an entire community. Since the recent suicides by students who have been victims of bullying, many school leaders now see the connection between bullying, disrespectful behavior, and teen suicide.

In this environment of increasing awareness of the importance of social and emotional challenges in schools, educational leaders also feel increased pressure to respond to competing demands for improved test scores, development of twenty-first-century skills, and serving more diverse learners. Addressing these issues one at a time can lead to institutional schizophrenia, with teachers and students feeling pushed from one agenda to another as each new idea is layered on top of the ones that were addressed before. The effect of such competing pressures and priorities can be overwhelming.

Each of these goals is worthwhile, but what is missing in most educational discussions about goals for our schools is a sense of *coherence*. It is not always intuitively obvious to all how these goals fit in a greater whole. For us, the glue that holds all these together is school climate. Instead of atomized initiatives and programs—one to address school safety, one to address bullying, another dedicated to academic classes, another on civic engagement, and another on technology—we envision an overarching focus on school climate and learning, under which each of these initiatives has an important place.

Schools that use school climate as a framework for bringing coherence to their school improvement efforts will better understand:

- The balance between emphasizing improved academic results and the process of achieving them
- The connections between school climate, emotional and physical safety of students, and learning
- How data collection on school climate can help a school set overall improvement goals and take focused action

- Best practices to simultaneously improve climate and learning
- The importance of student participation as partners and experts on school climate issues
- How a school can "help itself" by using a consistent process of engaging students and teachers in goal setting and problem solving around any issue

IMPLICATIONS FOR SCHOOL LEADERS, TEACHERS, AND STUDENTS

Imagine a world in which school climate and learning was the central theme of educational improvement nationwide. Imagine policy makers at the federal, state, and local levels actively supporting, even demanding, improvements in school climate in every school. This new and authentic No Child Left Behind effort would enliven schools, enlisting the spirit of service and love of kids that called educators to the profession in the first place.

What might be different in a world where school climate and learning was the organizing construct for school improvement?

- People would come first, not "the system." Structures and schedules would be designed around how to advance school climate and learning. Not every learning experience would have to fit in a forty-five-minute period, not every grouping of students would have to be the same twenty-five per room, not all learning would occur in the classroom.
- The curriculum would broaden, to embed the fundamental assets of service, teamwork, compassion, persistence, and making good choices within the learning context.
- Discipline policies would be less about punishment and more about restorative justice—rectifying the situation and incorporating both victims and perpetrators back into the system.
- Instead of "covering" the curriculum, teachers would be led to help students "uncover and discover," leading to a greater focus on learning than teaching. With real attention to the individual success of every child, teachers would be encouraged to try diverse methods to reach every learner. Expectations for students would vary less, but routes to learning may vary more.
- We would stop searching for the one best system or the magic bullet to solve our problems, and realize that sustained school improvement is an ongoing process. Schools would collect data, set goals, take action, assess impact, readjust direction, collect more data, and develop new goals and action plans. No unrealistic promises need to be made, nor will there be simple measures of success or failure.

Educators and students and communities will engage in ongoing, shared work to make their schools the best they can be.

- A wide range of stakeholders would be included in the process. Because school climate is so much about individual experiences and perspectives, the only way to be really effective is to include a diverse range of stakeholders in the process of change. Each individual is an expert on his or her own experiences of school climate and thereby a unique resource for evaluating and designing climate.
- By including a diversity of stakeholders in the process, we would enhance climate. Through shared work, relationships build, individuals are empowered, and everyone can feel like their voice is valued.
- Schools would feel less frenzied and haphazard—instead of jumping from one program or idea to another, there would be a commitment to sustained and cohesive change, capacity building, processes for continual improvement. This all falls under the banner of school climate—positive relationships, engaged learning, personalization, and empowerment—the foundation of safe schools and for high academic achievement.

Most significant, we are confident that attention to school climate and learning would result in schools being more effective—lower dropout rates, higher attendance, elevated efficacy, greater satisfaction, increased academic performance, and better development of twenty-first-century skills. These results engender a self-reinforcing, sustainable cycle of school improvement. Implementing a reliable, collaborative action research process leads to improved results and a more respectful climate. Increased organizational capacity in turn allows more refined focus on learning and further improvements throughout the school. This is not a fad or magic bullet solution; rather, it is the sustained but rewarding work of continuous improvement that all dynamic and successful organizations do to grow and improve over time.

CONCLUSION

We hope this book has helped provide you with useful tools, a deeper commitment, and expanded ability to bring your students, teachers, and community leaders to the table to improve school climate and learning. It is time to apply what we know works in schools to guarantee that every child finds school to be a dependable haven for learning—a place where each is safe, respected, known well by adults and peers, and challenged and supported intellectually.

There is no longer any doubt that school climate can either promote or inhibit a student's ability to learn effectively. There is also no doubt that our schools must make fundamental changes to remain relevant in the twenty-first century. These transformed schools we must develop will promote *both* personal development and rigorous, engaging academic learning as a balanced package; means and ends will both be priorities.

What we are proposing is not rocket science, nor anything that good educators have not known for years. What children learn depends on more than just long lists of standards or high expectations. Context matters—the extent to which students feel emotionally and physically safe, challenged and supported, and personally valued determines much about how they will do in school. In all the lofty talk about school reform and educational policy, it is easy to lose sight of the daily interactions among teachers and students that determine how well any individual does in school. Focusing our attention on the individual experiences and perspectives of students and teachers, by making them partners in school reform, is the key to transform their schools into safe, personalized, engaging learning communities that ensure every child finds success.

Thank you for taking the time to consider these ideas. Thank you in advance for the work you will do to bring them to fruition for your own students, teachers, and communities. Enjoy the journey.

BOOK STUDY QUESTIONS

1. What are the most powerful barriers that you face in transforming your school so that it can become a more personalized, engaging, rigorous environment for learning?

2. What assets can you draw upon for support in making the needed changes? Who are your potential allies for improving school climate and learning in your school, community, and profession?

3. What are the first steps you are committed to doing right now to improve school climate and improve learning for all students? What are you committed to doing over the long-term?

4. What are the three or four key ideas or strategies that you can take away from this book that will inspire and assist you in taking effective action to transform your school?

5. What will you do now?

Appendix A

From Violence to Empowerment:
A Respect Continuum

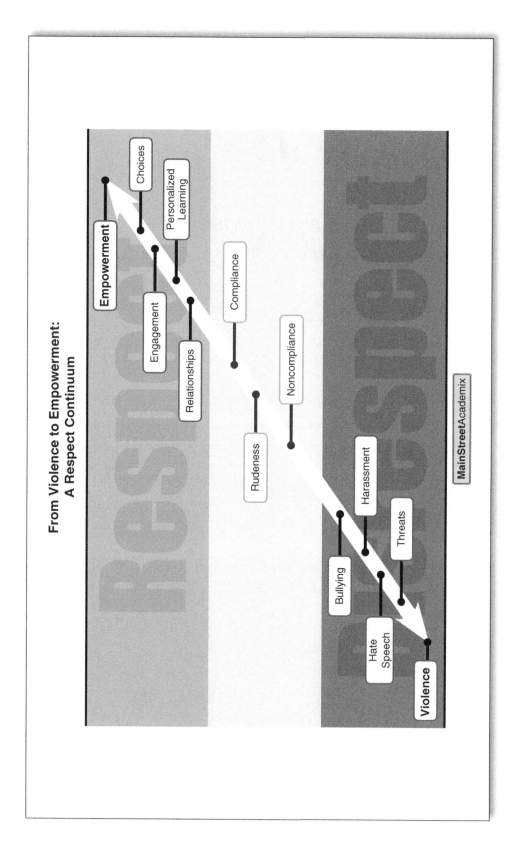

From Violence to Empowerment:
A Respect Continuum

MainStreetAcademix

Appendix B

Sample School Climate Data Summary

The Center for

School Climate & Learning

Sample School Climate Data Summary
High School/Middle School

	Students	Faculty	Gender		Race		Academic Aspirations	
			Male	Female	White	Diverse	College Bound	Other Plans
School Climate Standard 2: Policies & Student Supports								
Number of People Surveyed (n =)	267	45	131	136	206	61	184	83
When the principal or other administrators are told that a student is being bothered by another student they take action to stop it.	61%	82%	70%	52%	60%	69%	61%	50%
Our school provides help for students who are left out, rejected, or treated badly by others.	42%	62%	48%	38%	42%	42%	52%	43%
When teachers take action to stop bullying or harassment it really works.	21%	37%	28%	15%	21%	29%	22%	20%
School Climate Standard 3: Teaching & Learning Practices								
In my classes students have a chance to talk together, work together, and learn from each other.	74%	90%	75%	74%	75%	62%	75%	61%
Students are given opportunities to make choices about projects, papers, or research topics.	64%	92%	60%	68%	64%	60%	66%	51%
My teachers take time to ask me about my talents, interests, career and life goals, etc.	49%	72%	52%	46%	48%	42%	56%	45%
Teachers adjust their teaching styles based on my needs and interests.	39%	86%	42%	37%	40%	32%	41%	36%

	Students	Faculty	Gender		Race		Academic Aspirations	
			Male	Female	White	Diverse	College Bound	Other Plans
School Climate Standard 4: Safe & Welcoming Environment								
At my school, teachers treat other teachers with respect.	72%	64%	70%	75%	73%	67%	72%	72%
I feel safe at my school.	71%	86%	65%	77%	72%	63%	75%	62%
If I feel threatened at school, there is a safe person or place for me to turn to in order to get help.	63%	n/a	50%	77%	63%	50%	68%	55%
Teachers treat students with respect at this school.	61%	71%	61%	61%	63%	47%	61%	60%
School Climate Standard 5: Social & Civic Responsibility & Social Justice								
Students at this school have opportunities to work to make our community a better place.	75%	83%	77%	79%	77%	77%	80%	74%
Students are invited to offer ideas about improving our school.	66%	81%	64%	68%	68%	58%	67%	64%
Students treat others with respect, even if they are different or come from a different background.	46%	60%	50%	41%	45%	46%	48%	42%
Students step forward and help when they see other students getting bullied or harassed.	37%	10%	39%	34%	36%	44%	36%	40%

Note: All of the following tables show the percentage of each group who agreed with the statement.

Appendix C

Example of Student Goals and Evidence of Need: Elementary School Data (Grades 3–6)

All percentages represent those who responded positively to the SafeMeasures™ school climate survey questions, with 100% the best result. All quotes come from our qualitative database.

Goal 1: Adults will develop more effective consequences and support systems to address the effects of bullying and prevent bullying in our school.

Evidence: When adults try to stop bullying, it really works.

Low scores for students (46%) and faculty (47%).

Low scores for boys (53%) even lower for girls (39%).

Major differences in perceptions between college-bound students (68%) and noncollege-bound students (24%).

Evidence: Teachers are good at stopping bullying.

Low scores for students (42%) and large differences in faculty perceptions (79%).

Low scores for boys (48%) and large differences in perceptions of girls (36%).

Major differences in perceptions between racial groups, with white students (54%) and diverse students (30%).

Evidence: I (teachers) know what to do the help students who are being bullied.

Faculty confidence is high (89%) but student responses show they may be overconfident in their abilities to address bullying effectively.

Student Comments

"I would like to change the way kids treat other kids who have problems learning."

"I don't like the way some kids make fun of a kid if he is in a wheelchair or fat."

"We need teachers to do something about bullying when we tell them it's happening."

"I would take all the people who are bullies and let them know it's not cool to be bullied."

"Stop bullies . . . I get bullied a lot and wish that I had a chance to stop it from happening to me."

Goal 2: Teachers will make lessons more engaging so students are more excited about learning by learning more about their student interests, strengths, and learning styles.

Evidence: My teacher knows the things I like and am good at.

Low scores for students (41%) and major difference in perceptions between students and faculty (74%).

Large difference in perceptions between college-bound students (52%) and noncollege-bound students (30%).

Evidence: I feel excited about the things I am learning in school.

Relatively low scores for students (66%).

Large difference between perceptions of boys (58%) and girls (74%).

Evidence: Teachers give me choices about the things I learn. (Teachers: I give my students choices about the things they do in class.)

Relatively low scores for both students (38%) and faculty (40%).

Large difference between perceptions of college-bound (55%) and noncollege-bound students (21%).

Evidence: I use computers to help me learn at school. (Teachers: My students use . . .)

Low scores for students and large differences in student (21%) and faculty (91%) perceptions.

Student Comments

"My teachers are the *best* thing about this school . . . they are always nice to me and teach in a way we all understand."

"My teacher is funny and that keeps me awake."

"I like that we have SMART Boards and I wish students could use them more."

"I want to use art and drawing more."

"I would give kids a chance to work as fast or slow as they need to."

"I think kids should get a say about what they think about like the stories in the class and stuff."

Goal 3: Teachers will provide more opportunities for students to be active, responsible members of the school and community.

Evidence: At my school, students work to help the community.

Relatively low scores for students (44%) and large difference between perceptions of students and faculty (70%).

Evidence: Students are asked for their ideas about how to improve this school.

Relatively low scores for students (51%) and faculty (50%).

Evidence: Older students are kind to younger students.

Relatively low scores for students (67%) and faculty (65%).

Evidence: If a student is being bullied, other students try to make him or her feel better.

Relatively low scores for students (51%) and large difference between perceptions of students and faculty (80%).

Student Comments

"We need more group activities that help us to work together."

"I like it when some teachers let us use what we learn in class to do projects."

"I would change the way kids don't have a say in rules, activities, and other things we do."

"I would change how teachers are hired. Students should have a say in the teachers that are hired."

"I would change how students act with each other . . . I am new this year and the girls hurt other girls so much."

References

Adelman, H. S., & Taylor, L. (2005). *The implementation guide to student learning supports in the classroom and schoolwide: New directions for addressing barriers to learning.* Thousand Oaks, CA: Corwin.

Anderson, C. S. (1982). The search for school climate: A review of the research. *Review of Educational Research, 52*(3), 368–420. doi: 10.3102/00346543052003368

Baker, J., & Lynch, K. (1999). Equality studies: The academy and the role of research in emancipatory social change. *The Economic and Social Review, 1*(1), 41–69.

Bandura, A. (1986). *Social foundations of thought and action: A social cognitive theory.* Upper Saddle River, NJ: Prentice-Hall.

Bandura, A. (1997). *Self-efficacy: The exercise of control.* New York: W. H. Freeman.

Burns-Knight, M. (1992). *Talking walls: An illustrated description of walls around the world and their significance.* Gardiner, ME: Tilbury House Publishers.

Burns-Knight, M. (1997). *Talking walls: The stories continue.* Gardiner, ME: Tilbury House Publishers.

Caine, R. N., & Caine, G. C. (1997). *Education on the edge of possibility.* Arlington, VA: Association for Supervision and Curriculum Development.

Cohen, J., & Elias, M. (2010). *School climate: Building safe, supportive and engaging classrooms and schools.* Port Chester, NY: National Professional Resources.

Cohen, J., Fege, A., & Pickeral, T. (2009). Measuring and improving school climate: A strategy that recognizes, honors and promotes social, emotional and civic learning: The foundation for love, work and engaged citizenry. *Teachers College Record.* Retrieved from www.tcrecord.org/Content.asp?ContentId=15698

Csikszentmihalyi, M., & Larson, R. (1986). *Being adolescent: Conflict and growth in the teenage years.* New York: Basic Books.

Cumming, B. (2008). Inspired Teaching. *The Boothby Institute.* Retrieved from www.theboothbyinstitute.org/programs/inspired-teaching/

Dambrun, M., & Taylor, D. (2005). "Race," sex and social class differences in cognitive ability: Towards a contextual rather than genetic explanation. *Current Research in Social Psychology, 10*(13), 188–202.

Davis, S., & Nixon, C. L. (2011). *Initial findings from the Youth Voice Project: What we have learned about strategy effectiveness and peer victimization.* Unpublished Manuscript.

Dewey, J. (1998). *Experience and education.* New York: Touchstone. (Original work published 1938)

DuFour, R., DuFour, R., Eaker, R., & Many, T. W. (2006). *Learning by doing: A hand-book for professional learning communities at work.* Bloomington, IN: Solution Tree.

Durant, W., & Durant, A. (1935). *The story of civilization: The age of faith; a history of medieval civilization (Christian, Islamic, and Judaic) from Constantine to Dante, A.D. 325–1300.* New York: Simon & Schuster.

Edmonds, R. R. (1979). *A discussion of the literature and issues related to effective schooling.* Urbana: University of Illinois at Urbana-Champaign.

Farrington, D., & Ttofi, M. (2009). *School-based programs to reduce bullying and victimization.* Oslo, Norway: Campbell Systematic Reviews.

Florida Center for Instructional Technology (FCIT). (n.d.). *Using data to make decisions.* Retrieved from http://fcit.usf.edu/data/index.html

Freiberg, H. J. (1998). Measuring school climate: Let me count the ways. *Educational Leadership, 56*(1), 22–26.

Freiberg, H. J. (1999). *School climate: Measuring, improving and sustaining healthy learning environments.* New York: Routledge.

Freiberg, J. A. (2008, March). *Preventing the unimaginable.* Presented at the Governor's School and College Security Conference, Central Connecticut State University, New Britain, CT. Retrieved from www.sde.ct.gov/sde/lib/sde/pdf/pressroom/3_27_08_keynote.pdf

Fullan, M. (1993). *Change forces: Probing the depths of educational reform.* Levittown, PA: Falmer Press.

Fullan, M. (2001). *The new meaning of educational change.* New York: Teachers College Press.

Fullan, M. (2008). *The six secrets of change: What the best leaders do to help their organizations survive and thrive.* San Francisco: Jossey-Bass.

Hammond, C., Linton, D., Smink, J., & Drew, S. (2007, May). *Dropout risk factors and exemplary programs: A technical report.* Clemson, SC: National Dropout Prevention Center and Alexandria, VA: Communities in Schools. Retrieved from www.dropoutprevention.org/sites/default/files/uploads/major_reports/DropoutRiskFactorsandExemplaryProgramsFINAL5–16–07.pdf

Haney, C., Banks, C., & Zimbardo, P. (1973). Interpersonal dynamics in a simulated prison. *International Journal of Criminology and Penology, 1,* 69–97.

Inamdar, P., & Kulkarni, A. (2007) "Hole-in-the-Wall" computer kiosks foster mathematics achievement: A comparative study. *Educational Technology & Society, 10*(2), 170–179.

Jane Elliott's A class divided. (1968, April 5). [Video file] Video posted to www.youtube.com/watch?v=JCjDxAwfXV0 (2008, July 16).

Jennings, K. (2010, August). *Keynote address.* Henniker, NH: Center for School Climate and Learning. Retrieved from: www.necscl.org/2010/08/2010-conference-keynote-kevin-jennings/

Jensen, E. (2008a). *Brain-based learning: The new paradigm of teaching.* Thousand Oaks, CA: Corwin.

Jensen, E. (2008b). *Enriching the brain: How to maximize every learner's potential.* San Francisco: Jossey-Bass.

Lather, P. (1991). *Getting smart: Feminist research and pedagogy with/in the postmodern.* London: Routledge.

Lawrence-Lightfoot, S. (2000). *Respect: An exploration.* New York: Perseus.

Lewin, K. (1939). Field theory and experiment in social psychology: Concepts and methods. *The American Journal of Sociology, 44*(6), 868–896.

Maslow, A. H. (1968). *Toward a psychology of being.* New York: Van Nostrand.

Mitra, S., Dangwal, R., Chatterjee, S., Jha, S., Bisht, R. S., & Kapur, P. (2005). Acquisition of computing literacy on shared public computers: Children and the "Hole in the Wall." *Australasian Journal of Educational Technology, 21*(3), 407–426.

Moore, W. P., & Esselman, M. E. (1992, April 20). *Teacher efficacy, empowerment, and a focused instructional climate: Does student achievement benefit?* Paper presented at the annual conference of the American Educational Research Association, San Francisco, CA.

National School Climate Center. (2009). *National School Climate Standards: Benchmarks to promote effective teaching, learning and comprehensive school improvement.* New York: Center for Social and Emotional Education. Retrieved from www.schoolclimate.org/climate/documents/school-climate-standards-csee.pdf

Office of Special Education Programs (OSEP). (n.d.). *OSEP center on positive behavioral interventions & supports: Effective schoolwide interventions.* Retrieved from www.pbis.org

Office of Special Education Programs (OSEP). (2011). *School-wide PBIS.* Retrieved from www.pbis.org/school/default.aspx

Olweus, D. (1972). Personality and aggression. In J. K. Cole & D. D. Jensen (Eds.), *Nebraska Symposium on Motivation* (pp. 261–321). Lincoln: University of Nebraska Press.

Olweus, D. (1993). *Bullying at school: What we know and what we can do.* Malden, MA: Blackwell.

Palmer, P. J. (2007). *The courage to teach: Exploring the inner landscape of a teacher's life.* San Francisco: Jossey-Bass.

Pope, D. (2010). Beyond "doing school": From "stressed-out" to "engaged in learning." *Education Canada, 50*(1), 4–8.

Preble, W. K. (2003, Summer). From violence to empowerment: A continuum of respect and disrespect in schools. *New Hampshire Journal of Education, 4,* 1–4.

Preble, W. K., & Knowles, K. (2011). *Looking inside school climate: A review of school-based research.* Unpublished manuscript.

Preble, W., & Newman, A. (2006). *School climate improvement means higher academic performance in Sullivan County schools.* Unpublished report.

Preble, B., & Taylor, L. (2008). School climate through students' eyes. *Educational Leadership, 66*(4), 35.

Rivers, I., Poteat, V. P., Noret, N., & Ashurst, N. (2009). Observing bullying at school: The mental health implications of witness status. *School Psychology Quarterly, 24*(4), 211–223.

Sagor, R. (2000). *Guiding school improvement with action research.* Alexandria, VA: Association for Supervision and Curriculum Development.

Sagor, R. (2005). *The action research guidebook: A four-step process for educators and school.* Thousand Oaks, CA: Corwin.

Sarason, S. B. (1990). *The predictable failure of educational reform: Can we change course before it's too late?* San Francisco: Jossey-Bass.

Sherif, M., & Sherif, C. W. (1956). *An outline of social psychology.* New York: Harper.

Smith, L. (n.d.). *Liz Smith quotes.* BrainyQuote.com. Retrieved from www.brainyquote.com/quotes/quotes/l/lizsmith166861.html

Sparks, D. (2003). Interview with Michael Fullan: Change agent. *Journal of Staff Development, 24*(1). Retrieved from www.learningforward.org/news/jsd/fullan 241.cfm

StateUniversity.com Education Encyclopedia. (n.d.). *School climate—measuring school climate, school climate and outcomes, issues trends and controversies.* State University.com. Retrieved from http://education.stateuniversity.com/pages/ 2392/School-Climate.html

Tschannen-Moran, M., Woolfolk Hoy, A., & Hoy, W. K. (1998). Teacher efficacy: Its meaning and measure. *Review of Educational Research, 68*(2), 201–248. doi: 10.3102/00346543068002202

U.S. Department of Health and Human Services. (2001). *Youth violence: A report of the surgeon general.* Retrieved from www.surgeongeneral.gov/library/youth-violence/toc.html

U.S. Secret Service, National Threat Assessment Center. (2002). *Threat assessment in schools: A guide to managing threatening situations and to creating safe school climates.* (NCJ No. 195290). Retrieved from www.secretservice.gov/ntac_ssi .shtml

Vygotsky, L. (1978). *Mind in society: The development of higher psychological processes.* Cambridge, MA: Harvard University Press.

Wagner, T. (2008). *The global achievement gap.* New York: Basic Books.

Walberg, H. J. (1984). *Community influences on learning.* Oxford, UK: Pergamon Press.

Warner, G., & Shuman, M. (1987). *Citizen diplomats: Pathfinders in Soviet-American relations and how you can join them.* New York: Continuum.

Wessler, S., & Preble, W. (2003). *The respectful school: How educators and students can conquer hate and harassment.* Alexandria, VA: Association for Supervision and Curriculum Development.

Wiggins, G. P., & McTighe, J. (2005). *Understanding by design.* Alexandria, VA: Association for Supervision and Curriculum Design.

Index

CORWIN
A SAGE Company

The Corwin logo—a raven striding across an open book—represents the union of courage and learning. Corwin is committed to improving education for all learners by publishing books and other professional development resources for those serving the field of PreK–12 education. By providing practical, hands-on materials, Corwin continues to carry out the promise of its motto: **"Helping Educators Do Their Work Better."**

Made in the USA
Monee, IL
27 September 2021

78806566R00103